MW00800845

Ages 3-6 & 7-11

WORSHIP BULLETINS

for KIDS

Pew pencil activities

Fall & Winter

Rainbow Publishers®
www.rainbowpublishers.com

WORSHIP BULLETINS

Ages 3-6 & 7-11

BULLETINS

for KIDS

Pew pencil activities

Fall & Winter

Jeanne Grieser
Mary Rose Pearson

I dedicate this book with a thankful heart to my pastor Donovan R. Graber, who has eagerly and willingly supported my ideas and use of children's worship bulletins in our own church. I thank God for spiritual leaders and brothers like you. — J.G.

I dedicate this book to our beloved physician and "guardian angel," Dr. Richard Hunton, who has shown his love for God and for my family by watching over our health for 35 years.
— M.R.P.

WORSHIP BULLETINS FOR KIDS: FALL AND WINTER
©2003 by Rainbow Publishers, fourth printing
ISBN 1-58411-014-7
Rainbow reorder# RB38041
church and ministry/ministry resources/children's ministry

Rainbow Publishers
P.O. Box 261129
San Diego, CA 92196
www.rainbowpublishers.com

Illustrator: Helen Harrison

Printed in the United States of America

Table of Contents

Ages 3-6

Ages 7-11

Introduction

It might sound like a cliché, but children really are the future of the church. But you know that already if you have purchased this book! Congratulations for wisely valuing your children and their worship experiences. *Worship Bulletins for Kids* will help you show them that they are important and welcome to your church services. The activities will get your kids quietly learning about the Bible, allowing your church's adult parishioners to give their full attention to the worship service.

This book includes bulletins for ages 3-6 and ages 7-11. Simply photocopy two sheets back-to-back and fold! Kids can complete the bulletins with just a pencil, then take the sheet home for extended learning. In this book, you will find lessons from the Old and New Testaments and for Special Days. We recommend matching the bulletins to your pastor's sermon topics, if possible. Your church's ushers or greeters can distribute the bulletins to kids as they arrive for church. Or give them to Sunday school teachers to give to kids as take-home worksheets. If your church has a children's sermon time, consider distributing the bulletins as the kids return to their seats.

These bulletins are not intended to replace the worship experience, but to enhance it. God bless you as you seek to further His kingdom by ministering to children.

What Does God Teach Me?

Match the shapes. Write the letter on the blank.

___

___

V   E   L   O

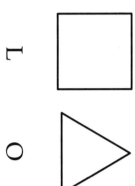

Answer:
love

God Teaches Me

Memory Verse:
Psalm 119:104 TLB   *Your rules can give me wisdom.*

....

In the Bible, God teaches us how to live and be happy.

Connect the dots.

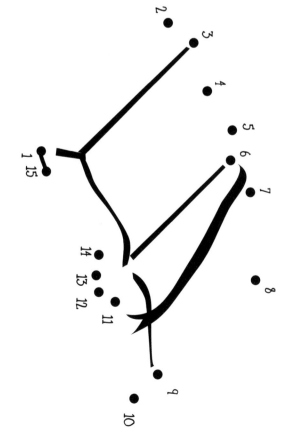

My Name: _____

A Big Fish

God taught Jonah obedience. Draw a  in the ocean.

Noah's Ark

God taught Noah faith. Draw an  in the water.

What Is It?

God created the animals. Connect the dots.

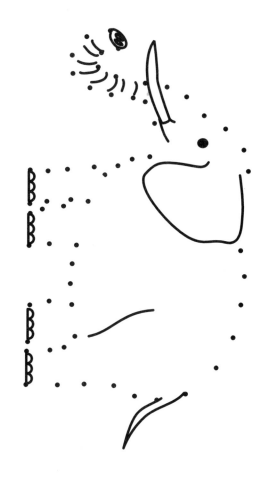

God's Creation Is Great!

Memory Verse:
Genesis 1:31 *God saw all that He had made, and it was very good.*

....

Circle the things God made.

My Name: _____

11

What Can You Create?

Using the shapes, make things God created. One is done for you.

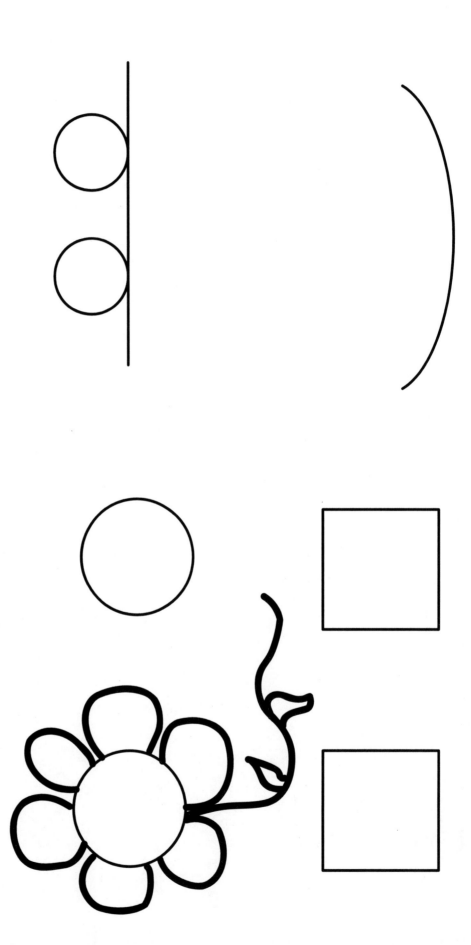

Your Favorite Season
....

Draw yourself outside in your favorite season. Remember to thank God for it.

Every Season Is Important

Memory Verse:
Genesis 1:14 *Let there be lights in the sky, and let them mark the seasons.*

....

God created the seasons. Seasons are important for plants and people. Circle the tree that shows your season right now.

My Name: _____

I Can Help

Take the cans to RECYCLE. Gather as many as you can along the way. God likes when we make good use of things.

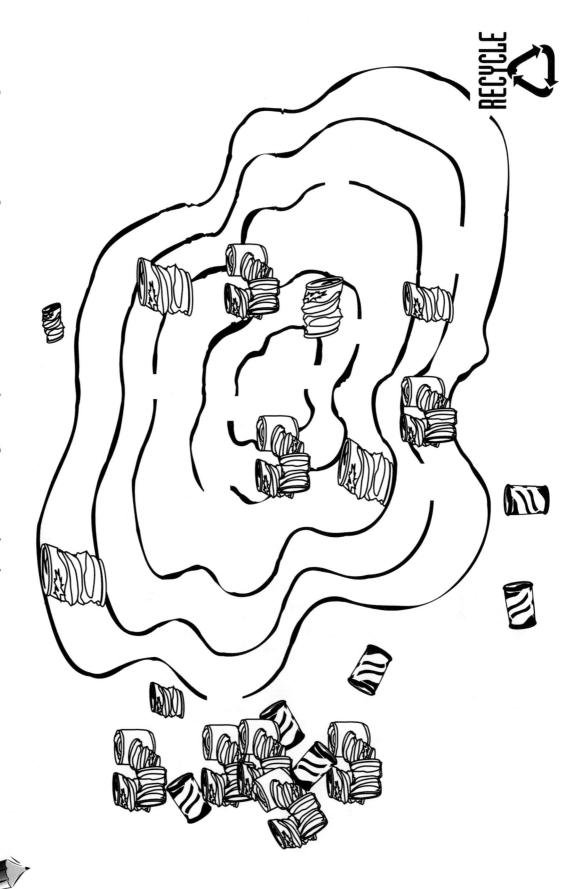

RECYCLE

My Family on Sunday

Draw a picture of what you and your family like to do on Sunday after church.

God Rested on Sunday

Memory Verse:
Genesis 2:2 *On the seventh day he rested from all his work.*

....

God wants us to rest on Sunday and think about Him.

Draw 2 windows and 1 door on the church.

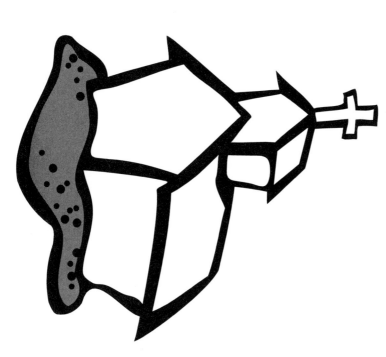

My Name: _____

My Face in Church

Draw your face when you are...

Singing

Listening

Praying

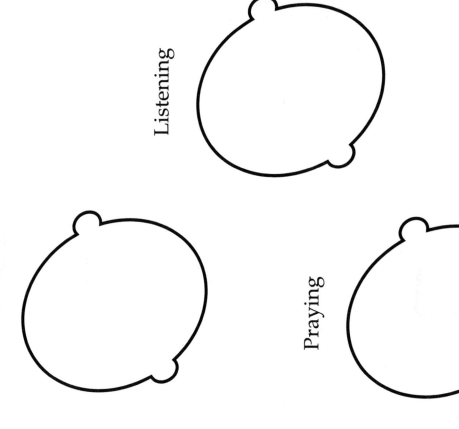

My Church

Draw the front of your church.

Pack Up

If God sent you on a trip like Noah, what would you pack?
Draw what you would take in the suitcase.

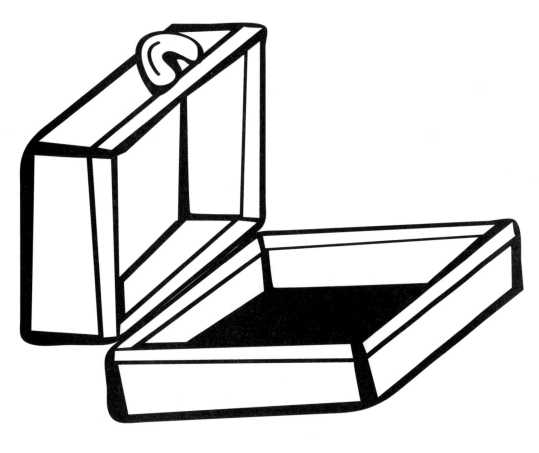

MY WORSHIP BULLETIN Ages 3-6

I Will Obey God

Memory Verse:
Genesis 6:22 *Noah did everything just as God commanded him.*

....

Noah loved and obeyed God.

Connect the dots.

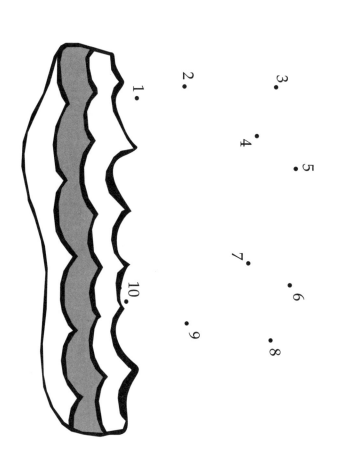

My Name: _____

How Many Animals?

Draw the second animal in each pair. Draw Noah and his family on the ark.

Sing and Play Music

Use the code to fill in the letters.

"M K ___ M ___ S ___ C

T ___ TH ___ L ___ RD."

Psalm 98:5

A =

E =

I =

O =

U =

Answer: "MAKE MUSIC TO THE LORD."

MY WORSHIP BULLETIN Ages 3-6

I Can Sing to God

Memory Verse:
Psalm 98:5 *Make music to the Lord.*

You can sing songs of thanks to God.

Color in the keys with an "x" on them.

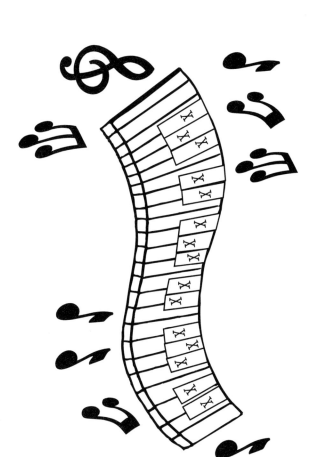

My Name: _____

21

I Can Play for God

Circle only the instruments.

My Prayer

Draw pictures on the hand of what and whom you pray for.

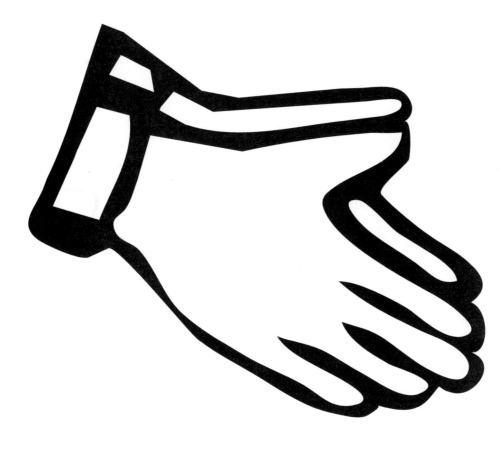

MY WORSHIP BULLETIN Ages 3–6

I Can Pray Anywhere

Memory Verse:
Proverbs 15:29 *The Lord...hears the prayer of the righteous.*

God hears your prayers no matter where you are.

Draw yourself praying in this picture.

My Name: _____

23

I Can Pray During The Day

Draw a sun in the sky.

I Can Pray at night

Draw a moon in the sky.

On a Boat

God wants families to love each other. This family likes to go on a boat. Follow the maze and help them go to the dock.

MY WORSHIP BULLETIN Ages 3-6

Families Are Special to God

Memory Verse:
Genesis 1:27 *God created...male and female.*

....

God created you and your family.

Draw a picture of your family.

My Name: _____

25

Families Play Together

Circle the things your family does together. Do these things make God happy?

I Learn About Jesus at Home

Draw a picture of how you learn about Jesus at home.

I Learn About Jesus

Memory Verse:

John 21:30-31 TLB *[Jesus' miracles] are recorded so that you will believe that he is...the Son of God.*

Tell yourself a story about each picture.

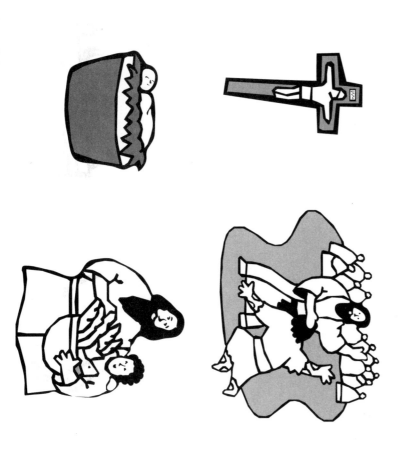

My Name: _____

27

Jesus Feeds a Crowd

Connect the dots to make the basket.

Jesus Turns Water to Wine

Connect the dots to make another jug.

God Said

Use the code to write the letters.

"TH__S __S MY S __ N,

WH__M I L__V__." (Matthew 3:17)

E =
I =
O =

MY WORSHIP BULLETIN Ages 3–6

Jesus Is Baptized

Memory Verse:
Matthew 3:16 *Jesus was baptized.*

Jesus was baptized in a river. He made God happy.

Draw flowers next to the river.

My Name: _____

29

Baptism in My Church

Draw a picture of your church during a baptism.

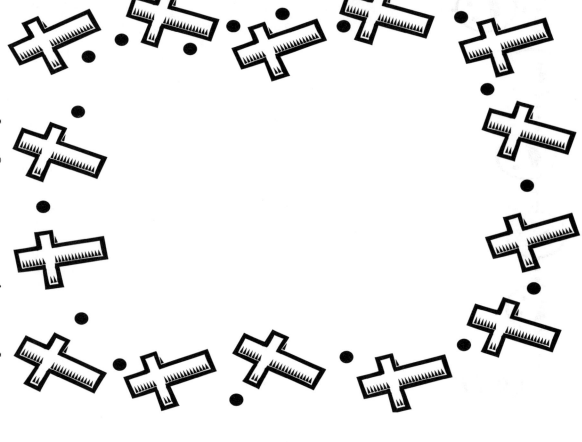

Following Jesus

Help the crowd find Jesus.

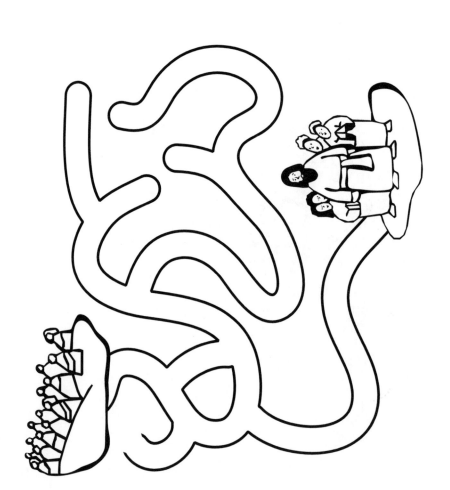

Be Happy

Do you know Jesus? Draw a happy picture of yourself.

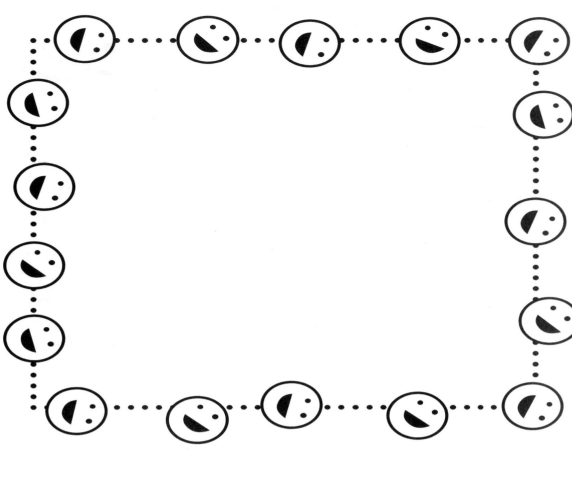

MY WORSHIP BULLETIN Ages 3–6

Be-e Happy

Memory Verse:
Matthew 5:12 *Rejoice and be glad.*

....

Jesus tells us to be happy. We can be happy because we know Jesus.

Decorate the word "happy."

My Name: _____

I'm Happy

Circle the pictures that make you happy. God wants you to be happy. Thank Him when you are happy.

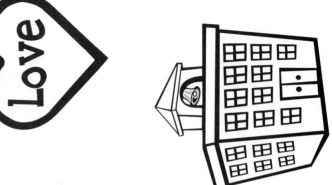

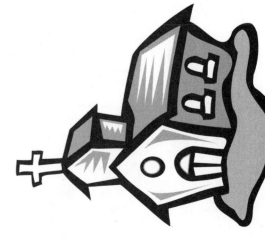

Are You Afraid?

Sometimes we are afraid. Draw a picture of what scares you.
Then draw a picture of what Jesus wants you to do.

MY WORSHIP BULLETIN Ages 3-6

Jesus Is with Me When I'm Afraid

Memory Verse:
Mark 4:40 *He said to his disciples, "Why are you so afraid?"*

....

Jesus and His disciples got into a boat. A terrible storm came.
Wind and waves tossed the boat. Water went into the boat. The
disciples were afraid.

Connect the lines. Draw in the sky.

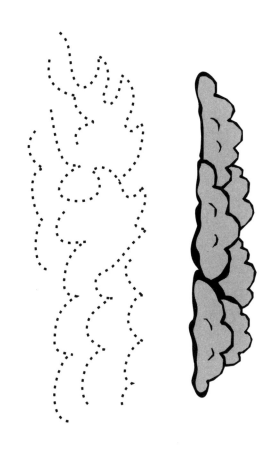

My Name: _____

Jesus Stood Up

He told the wind and the waves to be still. Everything was calm. He asked the disciples, "Why were you afraid?" The disciples could not believe that the wind and the waves obeyed Jesus. Draw Jesus' face and the disciples' faces.

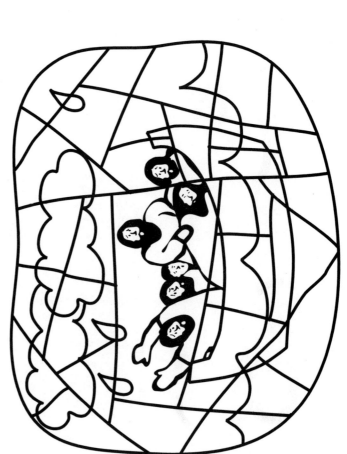

Jesus Was Sleeping

"Wake up!" the disciples cried. "We are going to drown! Don't You care?"

Find the hidden objects:

34

5,000 Were Fed!

Jesus fed 5,000 people with only 5 loaves of bread and 2 fish! Everyone was full. They put the leftover food in baskets.

Draw baskets on the ground.

MY WORSHIP BULLETIN Ages 3-6

5,000 Were Fed!

Memory Verse:
Mark 6:42 *They all ate and were satisfied.*

. . . .

The people listened to Jesus all day.

Draw their faces as they listened.

My Name: _____

Jesus Is Lost

Help Mary and Joseph find Jesus.

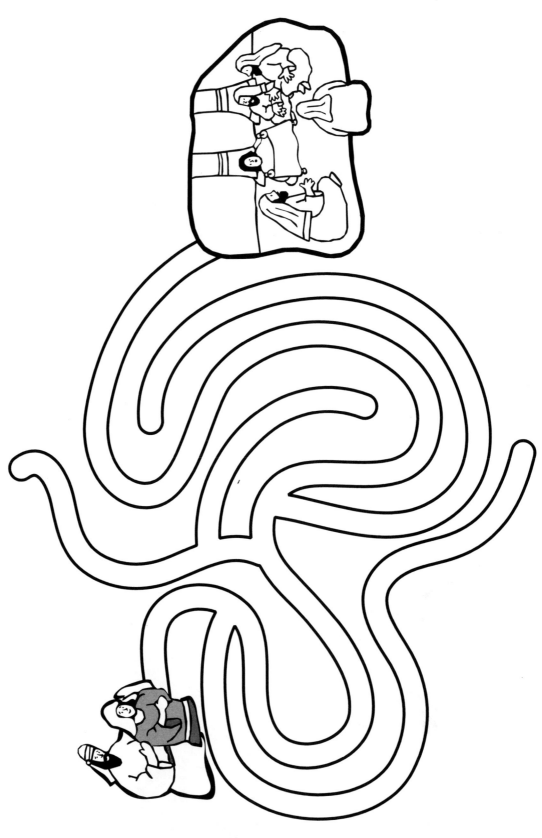

Love Your neighbor

Draw yourself showing God's love.

MY WORSHIP BULLETIN Ages 3-6

I Can Love My neighbor

Memory Verse:
Luke 10:33 *A Samaritan…came where the man was…and took pity on him.*

A man was traveling on a road when robbers hurt him. Two men saw the hurt man but they did not help him.

Connect the dots.

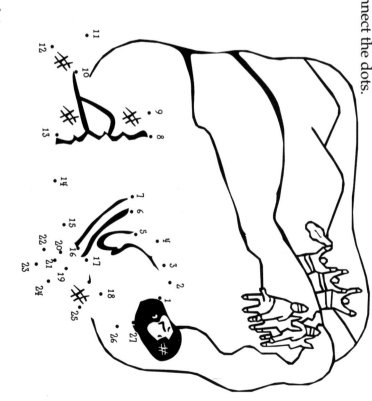

My Name: _____

To the Inn

The Samaritan put the hurt man on a donkey and took him to an inn until he was well. Help the Samaritan get to the inn.

The Hurt Man

A Samaritan saw the hurt man. He cleaned the cuts and put bandages over them.

Draw bandages on the hurt man.

40

What Did Jesus Say?

Use the code to fill in the letters.

"L ___ T TH ___ L ___ TTL ___

CH ___ LDR ___ N C ___ ME

T ___ M ___ ." — Luke 18:16

E =

O =

I =

Answer: LET THE LITTLE CHILDREN COME TO ME.

MY WORSHIP BULLETIN Ages 3-6

Jesus Loves Me!

Memory Verse:
Luke 18:16 *Let the little children come to me.*

Jesus loves children! Jesus loves you! Circle the large hearts that are the same.

My Name: _____

What Would You Say?

What would you say if you saw a miracle? Use the code.

O 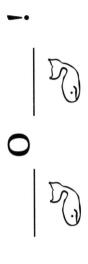 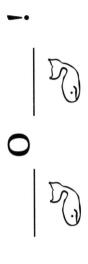 !

A  E O  E!

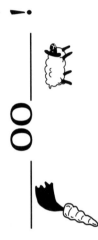 OO !

C =

L =

W =

S =

M =

I'm Amazed!

Draw the people's faces when they saw what Jesus had done.

44

A name for Jesus

Color in the shapes with a dot in them. Read the name for Jesus.

My Name: _____

Answer: Christ

MY WORSHIP BULLETIN Ages 3-6

My Name Is Special

Memory Verse:
John 14:6 *I am the way and the truth and the life.*

. . . .

*J*esus called Himself by many names. He tells us that He loves us and cares for us.

What is another name for Jesus? Match the shapes.

□ =S ○ =I △ =C □ =T ◯ =R ⬡ =H

△ ___ ◯ ___ □
◇ ○ □

My Name Is Important

Write your name. _____

How old are you? _____

I have _____ **brothers.**

I have _____ **sisters.**

My Hand

Trace your hand. Write your name on your hand. Write JESUS on your hand. Remember Jesus loves you.

Jesus Gives Me Many Things

Circle the pictures of what Jesus gives you.

MY WORSHIP BULLETIN Ages 3-6

Jesus Takes Care of Me

Memory Verse:
John 10:11 *I am the good shepherd.*

Jesus watches over us, like a shepherd watches his sheep.
How many sheep are in the pen? _____

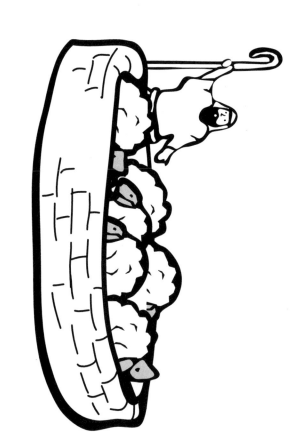

My Name: _____

Answer: 6

My Sheep

Draw one here. Thank God for sheep.

Sheep to Draw

Here is how you can draw a sheep.

1

2

3

4

48

I Can Show Love

Draw a picture of yourself showing God's love and peace.

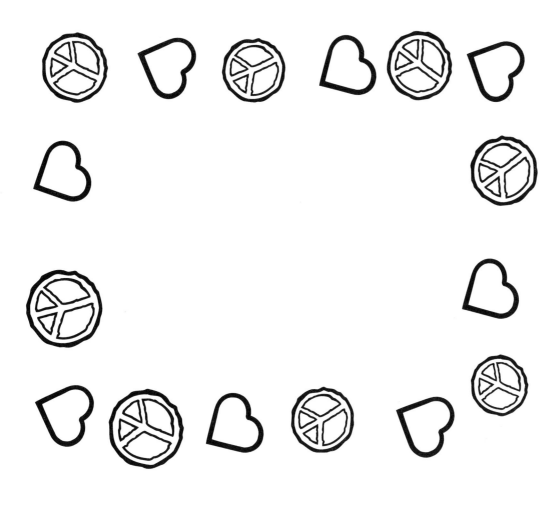

My Name: _____

I Will Live in Peace

Memory Verse:
John 13:34 *Love one another.*

Jesus tells us to love every person. We should live with peace in our hearts. Draw in the space below how you show peace.

My Hand Shows Love

Trace your hand. Draw a heart in the center.

Love one another.
John 13:34

Peace Puzzle

Find the words in the puzzle. Circle them.

LOVE   PEACE   JESUS

B L O V E A

K P E A C E

J E S U S A

Helping Out ·············

Katie obeys God. She is going to help her neighbor clean her yard. Circle what Katie should take.

MY WORSHIP BULLETIN Ages 3-6

I Can Help Others

Memory Verse:
Luke 6:31 *Do to others as you would have them do to you.*

·····································

We should always treat others with love like God treats us. Draw a line from the child with bad behavior to the child showing good behavior. Which behavior does God like?

My Name: _____

51

People to Help Us

God put people on earth to help each other. Draw a line from a problem to the person who could help.

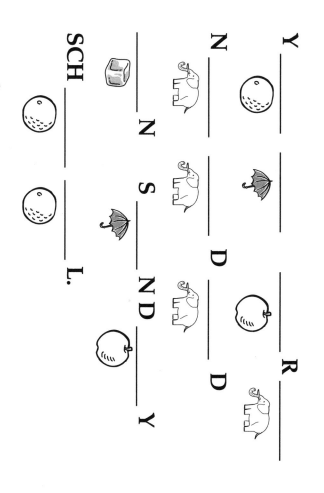

A note for you

Use the code to fill in the letters.

Y ___ R

N ___ ___ N ___ S ___ ND ___ D ___ Y

SCH ___ ___ L.

A = (apple)
E = (elephant)
I = (ice cube)
O = (golf ball)
U = (umbrella)

Answer: YOU ARE NEEDED IN SUNDAY SCHOOL.

MY WORSHIP BULLETIN Ages 3-6

Sunday School Kickoff

Memory Verse:
1 Corinthians 12:20 *There are many parts, but one body.*

You are important to your church. Your pastor and teachers like to see you in church each week. Write below what each child is doing in church.

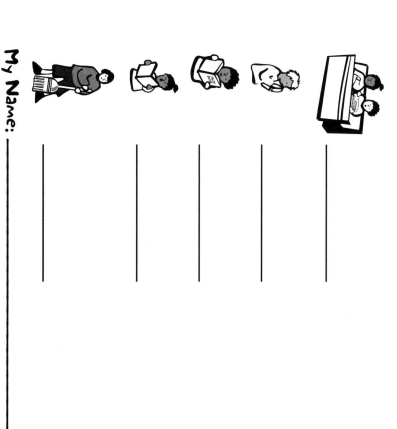

___

___

___

___

My Name: ___

In Sunday School

Draw yourself in Sunday School below.

You Are Special

Draw your face in the circle. Write your name on the line.

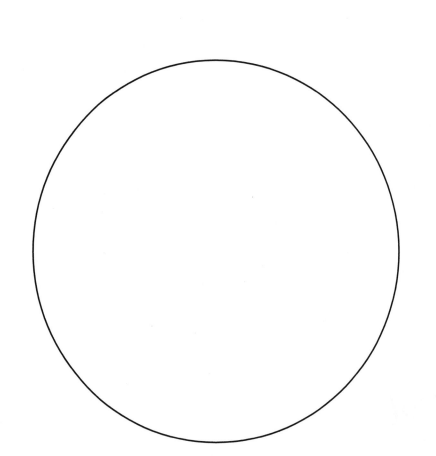

God Is with Us

God is with us when we are...

sad,

sleeping,

eating.

happy,

sick,

playing,

What are you feeling today? _____

Happy Thanksgiving

Memory Verse:
1 Thessalonians 5:18 **TLB** *No matter what happens, always be thankful.*

Thanksgiving season is here. We need to thank God for being with us and loving us.

Draw your favorite Thanksgiving food below.

My Name: _____

Give Thanks

How many of each thing below do you have? Write the number on each line. Remember to thank God for all He gives you.

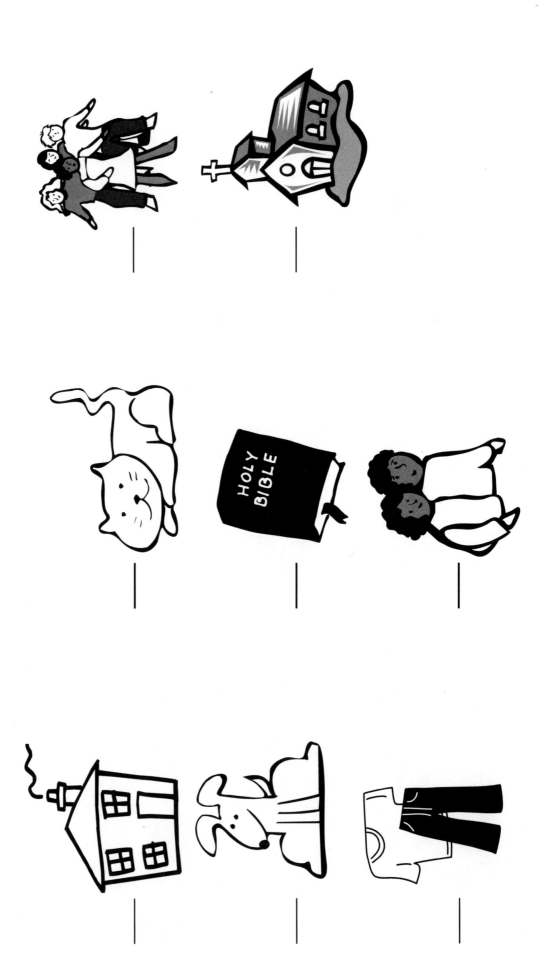

MY WORSHIP BULLETIN Ages 3-6

Advent: Jesus Is Coming

Memory Verse:
Isaiah 4:6 *For to us a child is born, to us a son is given.*

. . . .

Hundreds of years before Jesus was born, Isaiah said Jesus would be born. He gave people hope. During Advent, we look forward to Jesus' birthday. How many candles are on His cake?

My Name: _____

Jesus Is Our Gift
....

Connect the dots. Draw decorations on the picture.

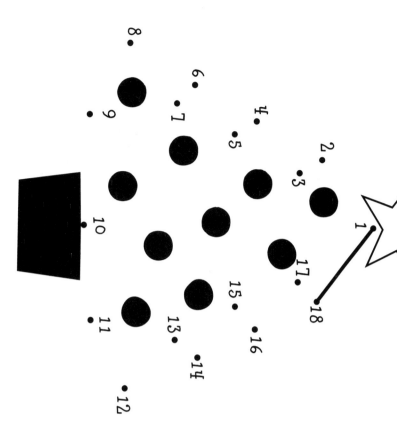

Who Is Coming?

Color in the squares that have a dot in them.

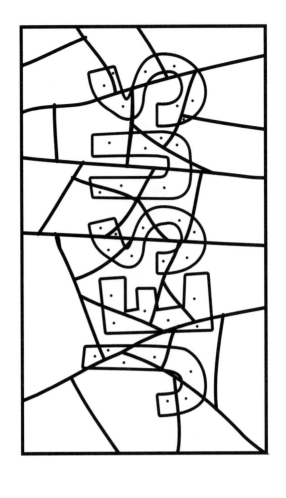

Advent Candles

Add a 🖊 to each candle.

My Christmas Day

Draw a picture of what you will do on Christmas Day. Don't forget to thank God for baby Jesus!

My Name: _____

MY WORSHIP BULLETIN Ages 3-6

Christmas: Jesus Is Born

Memory Verse:
Luke 2:7 *She gave birth to her firstborn, a son.*

....

Jesus was born. Mary and Joseph were happy. Circle Mary. Draw a ☐ around Joseph. Draw a ♡ around baby Jesus.

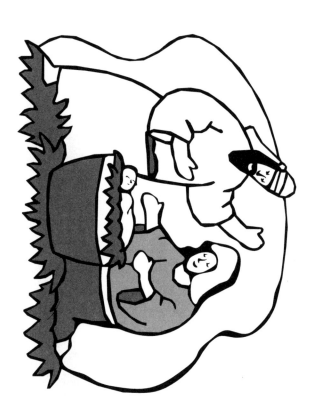

A Special Baby

Draw Mary and Joseph's faces. Draw Jesus in the manger.

Good News

Connect the lines to finish the birth announcement.

WHO
Jesus

TO WHOM
Mary and Joseph

WHERE
Bethlehem

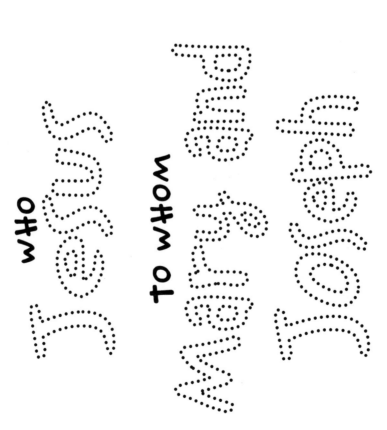

Christmas Songs

Match the shapes to fill in the letters.

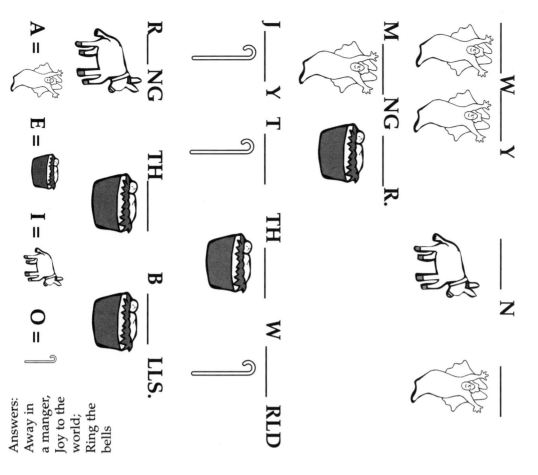

— W _ Y   — _ N   _ —

M _ NG _ R.

J _ Y T _ TH _ W _ RLD

R _ NG TH _ B _ LLS.

A = E = I = O =

Answers:
Away in
a manger,
Joy to the
world;
Ring the
bells

MY WORSHIP BULLETIN Ages 3-6

Christmas: A Big Announcement

Memory Verse:
Luke 2:10 *I bring you good news of great joy.*

....

Angels told the shepherds the good news. Jesus was born!
How many angels are in this picture?

_____

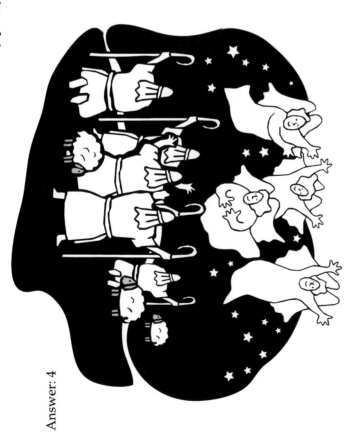

Answer: 4

My Name: _____

The Shepherds

What is the shepherd holding? Connect the dots.

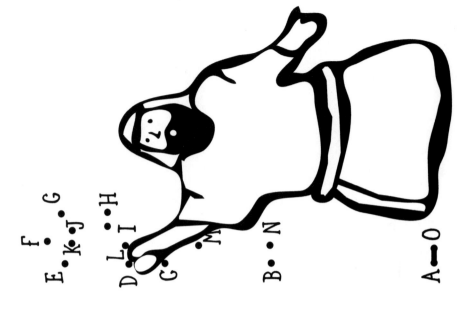

F
E • G
• K • J •
L • • H
D • I
G •

B • • N

A •—• O

M

The Messenger

Connect the dots.

The Christmas Story

Circle the pictures that are from the Christmas story. Draw an X on those that are not.

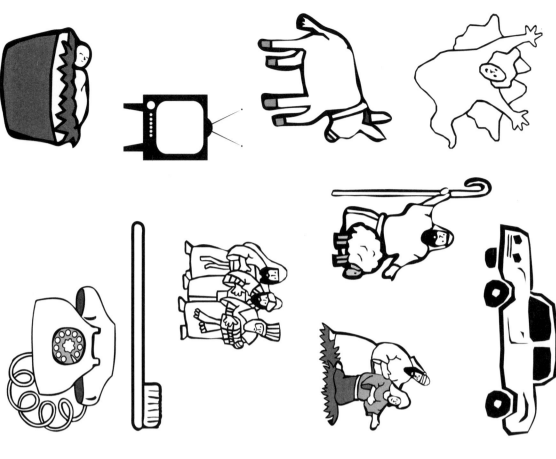

MY WORSHIP BULLETIN Ages 3-6

Christmas: Magi Worshiped Jesus

Memory Verse:
Matthew 2:11 *They saw the child...and worshipped him.*

Magi (wise men) came to see Jesus. They brought Jesus gifts. Draw the gifts

My Name: _____

63

My Gift for Jesus

What gifts would you have given to Jesus? Draw a picture below of your gifts.

Bringing Gifts

Draw the faces on the Magi.

A note for You ....

Follow the balloon string to the letter. Write the letter on the line.
What will you do for God in this new year?

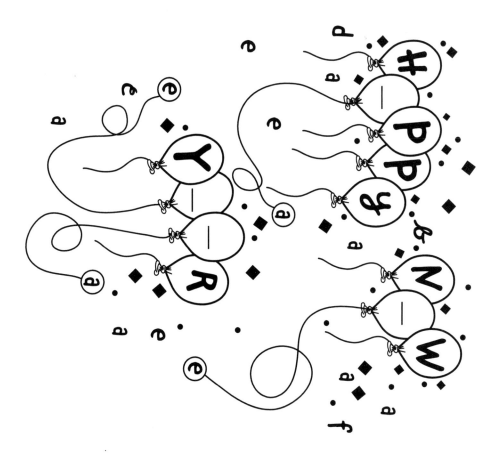

Answer: Happy New Year.

MY WORSHIP BULLETIN Ages 3–6

A new year!

Memory Verse:
Ecclesiastes 3:1 *There is a time for everything.*

....

God gives us each new year. What year is it now? Write the numbers on the lines.

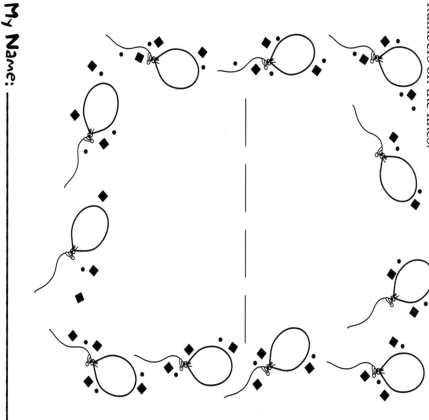

My Name: _____

A Time for All

God gives certain times for everything. Draw a line from the one on the left to its opposite on the right. One is done for you.

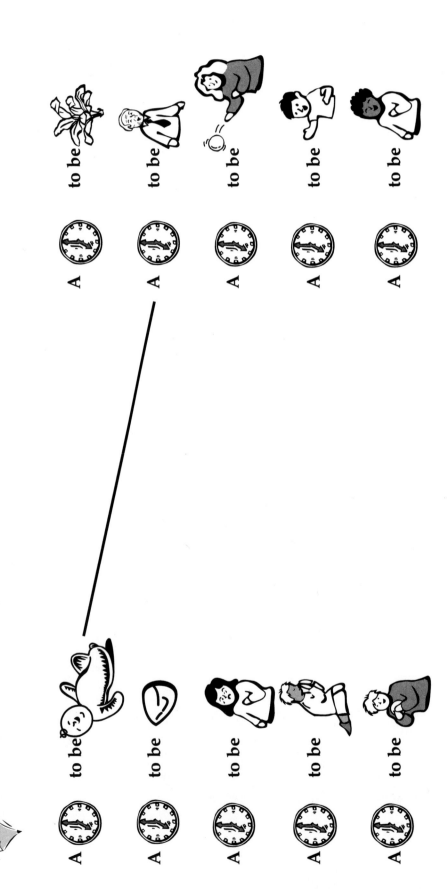

A ⏰ to be

A ⏰ to be

A ⏰ to be

A ⏰ to be

A ⏰ to be

A ⏰ to be

A ⏰ to be

A ⏰ to be

A ⏰ to be

A ⏰ to be

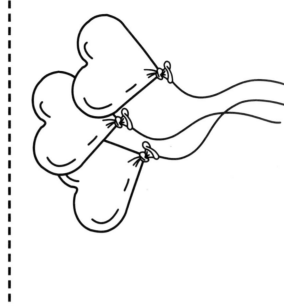

MY WORSHIP BULLETIN Ages 3–6

Happy Valentine's Day

Memory Verse:

1 John 4:7 *Let us love one another.*

Jesus wants us to love others. How do you show your love? Draw it below.

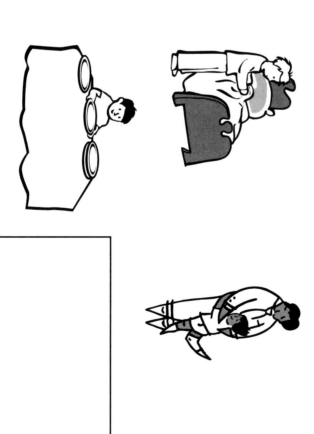

My Name: _____

67

Decorate the Word

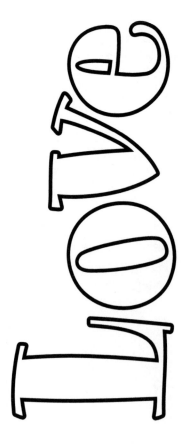

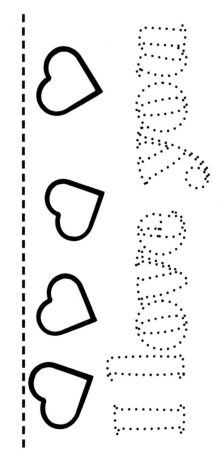

Use the next page to make a card. Connect the dots. Color the hearts. Sign your name. Draw on the blank side. When you get home, have someone help you cut out and fold the card. Give the card to someone you love.

68

Who Said or Did It?

You must not eat from the tree of the knowledge of good and evil.
Genesis 2:17

After God gave this command, Satan entered into a serpent and tempted Eve to eat the fruit. To tell the story, write each sentence number below the correct picture. The answers are inside.

1. Who said, "Do not eat the fruit on the tree of knowledge"?
2. Who said, "You will not surely die"?
3. Who ate the fruit?
4. What two frightened people hid among the trees?
5. Who named the punishment for the serpent and Adam and Eve?
6. Who had to crawl on his belly and eat dust?
7. Who had to work hard to make a living?
8. What two people had to leave the Garden of Eden?
9. Who stood by the garden gate to keep them out?
10. The Bible says, "All have sinned." If this means you, put this number under the boy or the girl.

____ ____ ____ ____ ____ ____

My Name: _____

My Worship Bulletin AGES 7-11

What Happened During Creation?

Memory Verse:
Genesis 1:1 *In the beginning God created the heavens and the earth.*

God has lived in heaven forever, but our earth had a beginning. God made it from nothing in six days. What did He do on each day? What did He do on the seventh day? Follow the paths from each day to what God did on that day. Write the words on the blanks in the correct order.

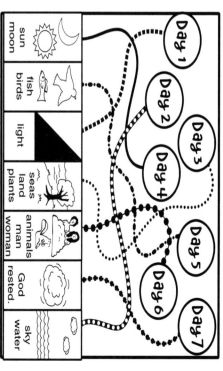

The Seven Days of Creation

1 ____ 2 ____ 3 ____ 4 ____ 5 ____ 6 ____ 7 ____

Creation Puzzle

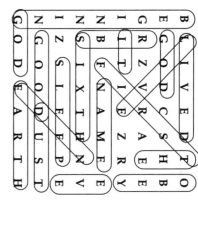

So God created man in his own image, in the image of God he created him; male and female he created them.
Genesis 1:27

Here is the story of the first two people God created. What were their names? _____ and _____. To complete their story, unscramble the letters in parentheses and write the word on the following line. Then circle those words in the puzzle across the page. You may go down, across or diagonally. Some words share letters.

In the (negibginn) _____ God created the heavens and the (heart) _____. Everything God made was (dogo) _____. (oGd) _____ made the (stirf) _____ man, Adam, from (stud) _____ on the (tishx) _____ day of creation. (odG) _____ told Adam to (mean) _____ all the animals He had created. God put Adam to (lepes) _____. Then He took one of Adam's (bris) _____ and made (vEe) _____ from (ti) _____. Adam and Eve (videl) _____ in the Garden of (neEd) _____. "Take care of (het) _____ garden," God said. He wanted Adam and Eve to (veol) _____ and (boye) _____ Him.

```
B   L   I   V   E   D   T   O
E   G   O   D   C   S   H   B
G   R   Z   V   R   A   E   E
I   I   T   I   E   Z   R   Y
N   B   F   N   A   M   E   E
N   S   I   X   T   H   N   V
I   Z   S   L   E   E   P   E
N   G   O   O   D   U   S   T
G   O   D   E   A   R   T   H
```

Answer Key

Answers: Adam, Eve, beginning, earth, good, God, first, dust, sixth, God, name, sleep, ribs, Eve, it, lived, Eden, the, love, obey.

Answers to front: 1. God, 2. snake, 3. Adam and Eve, 4. Adam and Eve, 5. God, 6. snake, 7. Adam and Eve, 8. Adam and Eve, 9. angel, 10. boy or girl

The Rainbow Promise

Will there ever be a worldwide flood again? God told Noah the answer when He put His rainbow in the sky. Find God's answer on the rainbow below. Put the words in their correct order to fill the blanks. Remember these words when you see a rainbow!

God said, "N _ _ _ _ _

_ _ _ _ _ _ _ _ _

_ _ _ _ _ _ _ _ _

_ _ _ _ _ _ _ _ _

_ _ _ _ ." (Genesis 9:15)

God always keeps His promises. You can count on it! Here is another of God's good promises to remember: "The Lord your God will be with you wherever you go." (Joshua 1:9)

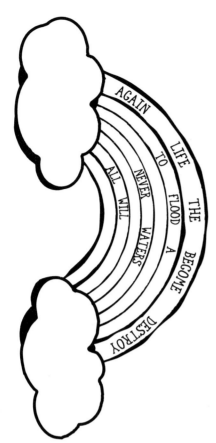

AGAIN LIFE THE
TO BECOME
NEVER FLOOD
WATERS A
ALL
WILL DESTROY

Answer: Never again will the waters become a flood to destroy all life.

Noah's Faith

Memory Verse:

Hebrews 11:7 *By faith Noah, when warned about things not yet seen, in holy fear built an ark to save his family.*

Noah built an ark by faith. Find and circle in the word search puzzle below all of the words in this definition of faith:

FAITH IS TAKING GOD AT HIS WORD AND ACTING ON IT.

```
F  A  I  T  H  R
M  C  S  A  I  E
A  T  P  K  S  W
O  I  T  I  I  O
O  N  A  N  D  R
S  G  S  G  O  D
```

Write the letters not inside circles here: _____
Unscramble them to finish this sentence:
GOD ALWAYS KEEPS HIS _____.

Answer Key

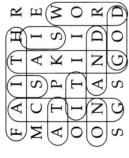

My Name: _____

71

Noah and the Big Flood

Fill the blanks in the sentences about Noah by unscrambling the letters in each group of letters on the opposite page. There will be one letter left over in each block.

1. God told Noah, "The people have become very wicked, so I will send a _____. You must build an ark for you and your family."

2. So Noah _____ an ark.

3. Noah took _____ of each kind of animal into the ark.

4. God sent rain for _____ days and nights.

5. The waters covered the _____.

6. Noah and his family were safe in the ark and did not _____.

Noah and the Big Flood

| 1. OOD LOF | 2. TUB LIB | 3. SAE RIP |
| 4. YYT OFR | 5. REE HAT | 6. WDN ROD |

Write the leftover letters in order on the blanks to answer this question:

Why did God save Noah and his family from the flood? Because Noah _ _ _ _ _ God.

Using the code, fill the blanks in these words in Exodus 24:7: "We will _____ _____ everything the Lord has
2,5 1,5

_____ ; we will _____ _____ _____ _____ _____ ."
1,4 3,4 1,6 2,5   1,5 2,4 3,5 2,6

	4	5	6
1	S	O	I
2	B	D	Y
3	A	E	Z

Remember, God will bless you, too, if you obey Him.

Abraham's Big Family

I will make your offspring like the dust of the earth, so that if anyone could count the dust, then your offspring could be counted.
Genesis 13:16

Abraham did not have any children when God gave him this promise. He grew very old. Still, God did not give him a son. At last, Abraham and Sarah had a son, Isaac. How old was Abraham when Isaac was born? Circle the correct number from each pair and write the circled number on the blank line. Add the numbers to find Abraham's age.

1. Number of days God created all things: 25 or 6? _____
2. Number of days God rested after Creation: 7 or 1? _____
3. Number of days and nights it rained in the worldwide flood: 600 or 40? _____
4. Number of books in the Old Testament: 39 or 100? _____
5. Number of Jesus' disciples: 12 or 3? _____
6. Number of true gods: 7 or 1? _____
7. Number of ways to become a child of God: 1 or 12? _____

Abraham's age when Isaac was born: _____ years old.

Total: _____

Unscramble the letters and write the words in the blanks:

Isaac's _____ (thirb) was a _____ (ramicel) of _____ (odG). The offspring of Abraham and Sarah are called _____ (sweJ). Today there are so many that they cannot be _____ (nutdoce). Did God keep His promise to Abraham? Yes _____ No _____

Answers: 6+1+40+39+12+1+1 = 100 years
birth, miracle, God, Jews, counted, yes

Abram's Life in Ur

Memory Verse:
Genesis 12:1 *The Lord had said to Abram, "Leave your country, your people and your father's household and go to the land I will show you."*

Abram lived in the big city of Ur when God told him to leave. What kind of place was it? Fill in each blank in the description of Ur with the letter that follows the one given. (A follows Z)

A B C D E F G H I J K L M N O P Q R S T U V W X Y Z

Ur was a $\overline{F}$ $\overline{Q}$ $\overline{D}$ $\overline{Z}$ $\overline{S}$ city on the banks of the Euphrates

$\overline{Q}$ $\overline{H}$ $\overline{U}$ $\overline{D}$ $\overline{Q}$. Huge $\overline{V}$ $\overline{Z}$ $\overline{K}$ $\overline{K}$ $\overline{R}$ surrounded the city. Ur had fine $\overline{G}$ $\overline{N}$ $\overline{T}$ $\overline{R}$ $\overline{D}$ $\overline{R}$, $\overline{S}$ $\overline{D}$ $\overline{L}$ $\overline{O}$ $\overline{K}$ $\overline{D}$ $\overline{R}$, and

$\overline{K}$ $\overline{H}$ $\overline{A}$ $\overline{Q}$ $\overline{Z}$ $\overline{Q}$ $\overline{H}$ $\overline{D}$ $\overline{R}$. But the people there

worshipped $\overline{H}$ $\overline{C}$ $\overline{N}$ $\overline{K}$ $\overline{R}$. They even sacrificed

$\overline{O}$ $\overline{D}$ $\overline{N}$ $\overline{O}$ $\overline{K}$ $\overline{D}$ to the moon god. Abram

$\overline{V}$ $\overline{N}$ $\overline{Q}$ $\overline{R}$ $\overline{G}$ $\overline{H}$ $\overline{O}$ $\overline{D}$ $\overline{C}$ the true

So God told him to $\overline{K}$ $\overline{D}$ $\overline{Z}$ $\overline{U}$ $\overline{D}$. What $\overline{F}$ $\overline{N}$ $\overline{C}$.

did he do? (See the next page!)

My Name: _____

73

Abraham Obeys God

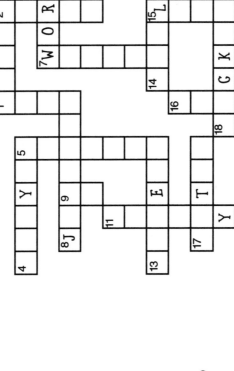

Abraham Obeys God

Here is the story of how Abram (later called "Abraham") obeyed God's command. Fit the words in all capital letters into the crossword puzzle on the opposite page. Some letters and one word are done for you.

ABRAM lived in the CITY of UR, where most people bowed down to IDOLS. GOD told him to leave that WICKED place and go to another LAND. Abram OBEYED God. He went to Haran, until his father died. Then, with his FAMILY, his servants and his animals, he traveled SOUTH. Maybe they WALKED or rode on CAMELS or DONKEYS. After a JOURNEY of 900 MILES, God told Abram to STOP in CANAAN. "This land is for you and your offspring," God said. So Abram BUILT an ALTAR and WORSHIPED God.

Answers for front:
great, River, walls, houses, temples libraries, idols, people, worshiped, God, leave

Isaac and His Wells

When Isaac grew up, he owned many sheep and cows. He dug a well to give them water. Some other men who owned cattle said, "That well is ours." Instead of quarreling, Isaac let them have it. He moved away and dug another well. Again the men claimed it, so Isaac moved and dug another well. This time the men did not bother him.

Numbered letters are on the stones of the well. Using the numbers beneath the blank lines, find the correct letters to fill the blanks. You will then have a word that describes Isaac.

Isaac was a $\underline{\quad}$ $\underline{\quad}$ $\underline{\quad}$ $\underline{\quad}$ $\underline{\quad}$ $\underline{\quad}$ $\underline{\quad}$ $\underline{\quad}$ $\underline{\quad}$ $\underline{\quad}$.
  1 2 3 4 2 5 3 6 2 7

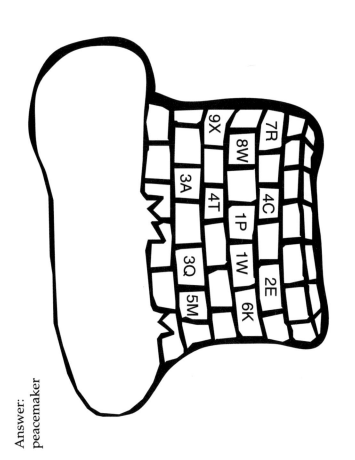

7R 4C 2E
8W 1P 1W 6K
9X 4T 3Q 5M
3A

Answer: peacemaker

A Test for Abraham and Isaac

Memory Verse:
Genesis 22:2
God said, "Take your son, your only son, Isaac, whom you love…Sacrifice him there as a burnt offering."

With this commandment, God gave Abraham a test to see if he would obey. It was a test for Isaac, too. What did they do? What did God do after the test? Cross out all of the z's in the sentences below to find the answers.

1. What did Abraham do?
zAbrahamzzobeyedzGodzandztookzzIsaaczwithzhimzzztozazz
mountain.zz.Heztiedzhimzzandzzzputzhimzonzzanzzaltar.zz
HezraisedzzhiszknifezztozsacrificezzIsaac.

2. What did Isaac do?
zIsaaczwaszazbig,zzstrongzteenager.zzHezcouldzhavezz
foughtzhiszzfatherzzbutzzhezdidn't.zHezobeyedzzGodzz
andzzhiszfatherzzandzzzletzhiszfatherzzputzhimzzonzthezzaltar.

3. What did God do?
zWhenzzAbrahamzzandzzIsaaczzobeyed,zGodzzsaid,z"Dozz
notzlayzazhandzonzthezboy.zzNowzIzknowzzthatzyouzfearzz
God."zzAbrahamzlookedzzupzzzandzsawzzazzzram,zcaughtzinz
zthezbusheszz,zandzhezzsacrificedzit.zzGodzzhadzprovidedzz
azzsacrifice.

(See answer key on next page.)

My Name: _____

75

A Bride for Isaac

Abraham told his servant to go to Haran and find a bride for Isaac. The servant found the girl God wanted Isaac to marry. He brought her back to Isaac. Go through the maze, taking the servant from Isaac and Abraham to Haran to find Isaac's bride and back to Isaac and Abraham. Pick up letters along the way to spell her name: _ _ _ _ _ _ _

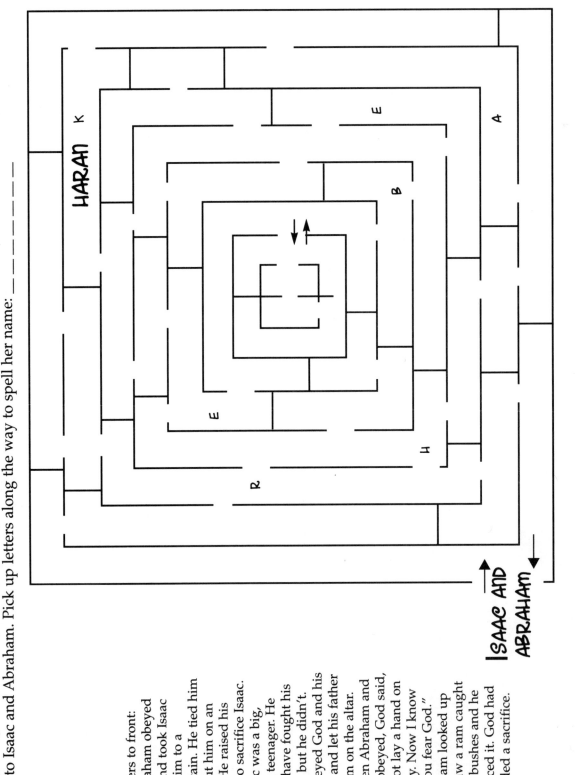

Answers to front:
1. Abraham obeyed God and took Isaac with him to a mountain. He tied him and put him on an altar. He raised his knife to sacrifice Isaac.
2. Isaac was a big, strong teenager. He could have fought his father, but he didn't. He obeyed God and his father and let his father put him on the altar.
3. When Abraham and Isaac obeyed, God said, "Do not lay a hand on the boy. Now I know that you fear God." Abraham looked up and saw a ram caught in the bushes and he sacrificed it. God had provided a sacrifice.

Sons of Abraham

He is the father of us all.
Romans 4:16

You are all sons of God through faith in Christ Jesus.
Galatians 3:26

Jacob's most important offspring was God's Son. God was His Father, and Mary was His mother. She was a descendant of Abraham, Isaac and Jacob.

Have you sung "Father Abraham"? The song says that Father Abraham has many sons. It goes on to say, "I am one of them, and so are you." Were you born a Jew? If not, how can you be a son or daughter of Abraham?

Add or subtract letters to find some answers from the Bible.

Abraham believed in ___ ___ ___, so he was
f+1 n+1 b+2

called a ___ ___ ___ of God. When we believe
u-2 l+3 m+1

in Jesus as Savior, we become ___ ___ ___ ___ of God. We
f-3 g+1 g+2 p-4 c+1 s-1 c+2 m+1

are Abraham's sons by: ___ ___ ___ ___ .
g-1 d-3 h+1 r+2 j-2

Answers: God, Son, children, faith

The Angry Twin Brother

Memory Verse:

Genesis 27:41 *Esau held a grudge against Jacob because of the blessing his father had given him.*

Isaac had twin sons, Esau and Jacob. Firstborn Esau was supposed to inherit most of his father's wealth and get a special blessing. Jacob wanted those things. He tricked Esau, got the inheritance and fooled his father to get Esau's special blessing. What did Esau say he would do after their father died?

To find the answer, travel through the maze, correctly following the letters in "THEN I WILL."

Answer: KILL JACOB

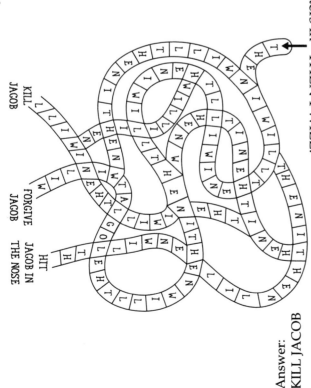

KILL	FORGIVE	HIT
JACOB	JACOB	JACOB IN
		THE NOSE

My Name: _____

77

Jacob's New Name

God gave Jacob a new name. To find it, write the letter that is missing from the second word of each pair below. Going down, write those letters in the blanks in the sentences.

In PAIR but not in RAP: ——
In STEAM but not in MATE: ——
In PARCEL but not in PLACE: ——
In BAIT but not in BIT: ——
In TRACE but not in CART: ——
In ALTER but not in TEAR: ——

Jacob's new name was —— —— —— —— —— —— .

Jacob had twelve sons and one daughter. Today his offspring (descendants) are so many they can't be counted. They are called by his new name. They are:
—— —— —— —— —— —— ITES.

Find another name for them in this puzzle:
In JEST but not in SET: ——
In TONE but not in NOT: ——
In TOWER but not in ROTE: ——
In STEAL but not in LATE: ——

Jacob's big family is also called —— —— —— —— .

Jacob Runs for His Life

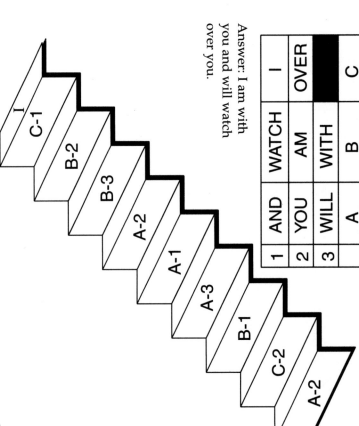

When he reached a certain place, he stopped for the night because the sun had set.
Genesis 28:11

When Jacob learned what Esau planned to do to him, he ran for his life. He went to sleep and had a dream about a stairway that reached from earth to heaven. Angels went up and down on it, and God was above it. God talked to Jacob. Using the code, write on the correct step the words of one promise God gave to Jacob. Go from top to bottom. The first one is done for you.

Steps (top to bottom): I C-1, B-2, B-3, A-2, A-1, A-3, B-1, C-2, A-2

	1	2	3
1	AND	WATCH	I
2	YOU	AM	OVER
3	WILL	WITH	■
	A	B	C

Answer: I am with you and will watch over you.

78

Joseph's Special Gift

Memory Verse:
Genesis 37:3 *Israel loved Joseph more than any of his other sons, because he had been born to him in his old age.*

What special gift did Israel (Jacob) give Joseph? Draw a picture of it by following the numbered dots.

My Name: _____

Joseph Is Faithful

So Pharaoh said to Joseph, "I hereby put you in charge of the whole land of Egypt."
Genesis 41:41

Joseph was put in a cistern and sold as a slave. He served an Egyptian master. He was put in prison for something he didn't do. Why did Joseph then get to be in charge of the whole land of Egypt? Because he was faithful to God. Trace a line from the bottom of the maze to the top, picking up the letters FAITHFUL, in order, as you go up, down, right or left. Hint: You will spell FAITHFUL five times.

End

F A I T H U L
L U F H U I H F
F A I T H I H A
L U F H I A F
F I L F T I A F
A H T A F U L
A U L I U L F A
L U L I U L F A
A H T H F A T I
F A I A U T L T

Begin

How to Get Rid of Jealousy

Love is patient, love is kind. It does not envy.
1 Corinthians 13:4

Fill in the blanks with the letter of the alphabet that follows the one given:

Another word for jealousy is __ __ __ __ .
                                D M U X

We will not __ __ __ __ someone if we truly
            D M U X
__ __ __ him or her.
K N U D

Shade all the squares that have a Z below.

Z	X	X	Z	Z	Z	X	Z	Z	X	X	Z	Z
Z	X	X	Z	X	X	Z	X	Z	X	X	Z	X
Z	X	X	Z	X	Z	X	Z	X	Z	X	X	X
Z	X	X	Z	X	Z	X	Z	X	X	X	Z	X
Z	Z	Z	Z	Z	Z	Z	X	Z	X	X	Z	Z

What word did you make? _____

Write the names of three people to whom you will try to show more love and no envy:

_____

Joseph's Troubles

When the Midianite merchants came by, his brothers pulled Joseph up out of the cistern and sold him for twenty shekels of silver to the Ishmaelites, who took him to Egypt.
Genesis 37:28

Why did Joseph's brothers put Joseph in a cistern and then sell him as a slave? Find the answer by shading these squares:

Row A: 1, 3, 4, 6, 7, 8

Row B: 1, 2, 3, 5, 6, 7, 8

Row C: 1, 2, 4, 5, 6, 7

Row D: 2, 3, 4, 5, 7, 8

	1	2	3	4	5	6	7	8
A	K	L	T	M	O	B	N	Q
B	D	C	F	E	H	G	P	V
C	Y	R	S	G	I	W	T	A
D	J	D	X	Y	B	U	Z	C

Write the remaining letters here: _____

Unscramble the letters and fill in the blank: Joseph's brothers were _____ of him.

Escape from Egypt

At last, Pharaoh let the Jews leave Egypt. When they came to the Red Sea, they discovered that Pharaoh's soldiers were chasing them in chariots. What happened next?

Use the code below to compute the math problems and find the right letters. Example: O(3)-R(2)=1. 1 is D.

God divided the waters so the Jews could cross

on __ __ __ __ __ __ __ __ .
    O-R D+D L+N R+O W-D O+D N-O

Pharaoh and his chariots followed. God sent the waters back, and they all

__ __ __ __ __ __ __ .
N-O D+D L-R Y-D R+R Y-O L-N

Then the Jews sang and praised __ __ __ .
                             E+N E-O W-A

CODE
1=D 3=O 5=L 7=A 9=Y
2=R 4=N 6=E 8=W 10=G

Answers: dry land, drowned, God

Baby Moses Is Rescued

Memory Verse:

Hebrews 11:23 *By faith, Moses' parents hid him for three months after he was born, because they saw he was no ordinary child.*

Choose the correct words from the list to fill the blanks in the sentences. Four words are not needed. See answers on page 2.

River   daughter   bad   kill   nurse
hid   sister   fine   crying   mother   lake
bathe   watched   steal   basket   sorry   wife

1. Pharaoh said he would _____ all the baby boys born to Jewish parents.

2. When baby Moses was born, he was a _____ child.

3. His mother _____ him for three months.

4. When she could not do that any longer, she put him in a basket in the Nile.

5. Miriam, Moses' big _____, _____ stood off at a distance and _____ him.

6. Pharaoh's _____ came to the Nile to _____.

7. She saw the _____ and asked a slave to get it.

8. She opened the basket and saw that the baby was _____. She felt _____ for him.

9. She let Miriam take Moses to a _____ until he was older. Miriam took him to her _____.

My Name: _____

Ten Plagues on Egypt

I will stretch out my hand and strike the Egyptians with all the wonders that I will perform among them. After that, he will let you go.
Exodus 3:20

What ten terrible plagues did God send on Egypt before Pharaoh would let the Jews go? Fill in the blanks in the sentences and fit the words into the crossword puzzle.

1. Water turned to _____ (3 down).
2. _____ (4 across) jumped in houses and everywhere.
3. The dust turned into buzzing _____ (5 down).
4. Swarms of _____ (4 down) covered everything.
5. The animals _____ (7 across) from a bad disease.
6. Sore _____ (3 across) covered people and animals.
7. _____ (2 down) chewed up the crops.
8. Icy _____ (1 down) destroyed the remaining crops.
9. The daylight turned into _____ (6 across).
10. All Egypt mourned the _____ (8 across) of their firstborn children.

God Speaks to Moses

Go. I am sending you to Pharaoh to bring my people the Israelites out of Egypt.
Exodus 3:10

God spoke these words to Moses from a burning bush. He worked a miracle to show Moses that He really was God. What was the miracle? Connect the dots in the top set first, then connect the bottom set.

Moses'

became a

82

Fiery Snakes!

Then the Lord sent venomous snakes among them; they bit the people and many Israelites died.
Numbers 21:6

In the desert, God gave the Jews manna to eat. They complained about God's food, so He sent snakes to bite them. Then He told Moses to put a brass snake on a pole. The people who looked at it were healed. Draw a line through the maze of snakes so the man with the bite can get to the pole.

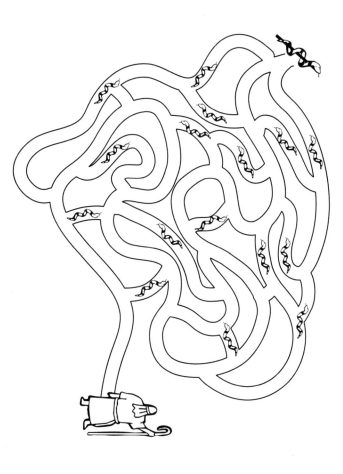

The Jews in the Desert

Memory Verse:
nehemiah 9:21 *For forty years you sustained them in the desert; they lacked nothing.*

. . . .

When the Jews escaped from Egypt, God led them through the desert with a cloud by day and a pillar of fire by night to light their way. How could more than two million people find food to eat and water to drink in the dry desert?

Unscramble these letters to find the answer and write them on the footprints: OGD OKTO REAC FO HEMT.

Answer: God took care of them.

My Name: _____

83

God Gives the Commandments

And God spoke all these words: "I am the Lord your God, who brought you out of Egypt, out of the land of slavery."
Exodus 20:1-2

A thick cloud hung over Mount Sinai. Lightning flashed and thunder rumbled. "Come to the foot of the mountain," Moses told the people. The frightened crowd came near. The Lord descended on Mount Sinai in fire, smoke billowed up and the mountain trembled. The Lord then said the words of the Commandments.

Draw lines to match the beginnings and endings of the Commandments. Cross out the phrases that do not belong.

1. You shall have no other   the name of the Lord.
2. You shall not make   father and mother.
3. You shall not chew   an idol.
4. You shall not misuse   Day to keep it holy.
5. Remember the Sabbath   bubble gum.
6. Honor your   murder.
7. You shall not watch   your neighbor's…
8. You shall not   gods before me.
9. You shall not commit   horror movies
10. You shall not   steal.
11. You shall not give   adultery.
12. You shall not covet   false testimony.

Food and Drink in the Desert

What kind of food did God give the Jews? Where did the water come from? Circle the word in each set that does not belong. Write it on the line with the same number.

1	2	3	4	5
dogs	ham	girl	Day	quails
cats	ground	boy	pencil	sun
manna	eggs	Sabbath	paper	moon

6	7	8	9
mother	yellow	water	trees
flew	red	shoes	rock
father	low	socks	flowers

1. Six days a week, God put _____ on the _____ .
   1   2

2. On the sixth day, there was enough _____ for the _____ .
   5   1

   _____ _____ .
   3   4

3. For their meat, God sent _____ that _____ _____ .
                             5   6   7

4. Two times God provided _____ from a _____ .
                          8   9

84

A Blow Out

The Israelites used blasts from horns to alert the people about different events. Although the horns used by the priests at the wall of Jericho were made from ram's horns, some horns were made from silver.

Shade in with a pencil all the areas that contain a letter from the words RAM'S HORNS or SILVER to find another name for the horns the priests blew.

Another name for the horn was a _____.

Answer: Trumpet

The Spies Enter Canaan

Memory Verse:

numbers 13:1 *The Lord said to Moses, "Send some men to explore the land of Canaan, which I am giving to the Israelites. From each ancestral tribe send one of its leaders."*

Twelve Jewish men sneaked in to explore the land God had given to them. When they returned, they gave a glowing report of the land. "It flows with milk and honey!" they said. They showed some of the fruit of the land. "We cannot go in and possess it," some of the men said. "There are giants in the land." What did they say they were like compared to the giants? Write the letter missing from each set. Then draw some of the creatures around the giant.

```
C D E F H I  ___
P Q S T U V  ___
X Y Z B C D  ___
O P Q R T U  ___
R T U V W X  ___
C D E F G I  ___
L M N P Q R  ___
M N O Q R S  ___
N O Q R S T  ___
A B C D F G  ___
P Q S T U V  ___
R T U V W X  ___
```

Answer: grasshoppers

My Name: _____

85

The Battle of Jericho

Then the Lord said to Joshua, "See, I have delivered Jericho into your hands."
Joshua 6:2

The first city in Canaan that Joshua and his soldiers had to conquer was Jericho. But how did they get past the big, thick walls of the city? Use the code below to fill in the blanks and discover what God did when the Israelites obeyed Him. Look for the letter in the puzzle in the code box, then write the letter above or below it.

N	O	P	Q	R	S	T	U	V	W	X	Y	Z
M	L	K	J	I	H	G	F	E	D	C	B	A

The Jews __ __ __ __ __ __ __ around Jericho once a
N Z I X S V W

day for __ __ __ days. __ __ __ __ priests blew
H R C   H V E V M

their __ __ __ __ __ . On the __ __ __ __ __ __ __ day
S L I M H   H V E V M G S

they __ __ __ __ __ __ __ around __ __ __ __ __
N Z I X S V W   H V E V M

times. The priests blew their __ __ __ __ __ . The
S L I M H

people __ __ __ __ __ __ __ , and down came the
H S L F G V W

__ __ __ __ __ !
D Z O O H

Answers: marched, six, seven, horns,
seventh, marched, seven, horns, shouted,
walls

Who Said It?

When the spies gave their report, not all of them thought they could conquer the enemies in Canaan. Some said, "Let's go!" Others said, "No!" From the two arrows, follow these two sayings to find who said each. The paths cross in one place, where they share a letter.

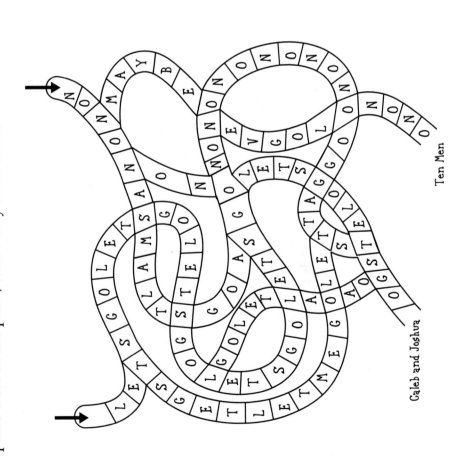

Caleb and Joshua

Ten Men

Answers: "Let's go!" — Caleb and Joshua;
"No!" — ten men

When Trouble Comes

God is our refuge and strength, an ever-present help in trouble.
Psalm 46:1

Caleb faced many troubles. He could have been afraid and given up. But he kept going. He believed God would $\underline{\quad}$ $\underline{\quad}$ him out of his troubles.
1   2

Follow each line from a cloud to a letter inside a sun. Write the letter where it belongs above.

$\underline{\ }$ $\underline{\ }$ $\underline{\ }$ $\underline{\ }$ $\underline{\ }$
3   4   5   6   7

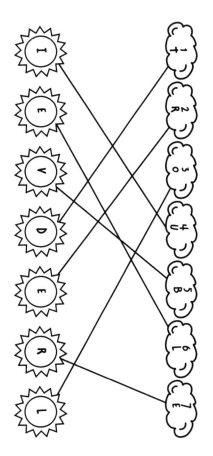

Are you afraid to stand up for what's right? Do you think you may get in trouble with other kids if you do? Stay true to God, no matter what happens. Remember, God is on your side. He will be with you and help you. Nothing is too hard for Him.

Answer: deliver

My Name:

A Brave Soldier

Memory Verse:
Joshua 14:9
On that day Moses swore to me, "The land on which your feet have walked will be your inheritance and that of your children forever, because you have followed the Lord my God wholeheartedly."

Caleb said the words above. He was one of the spies who went into Canaan to see what it was like. Ten spies were afraid of the giants. Joshua and Caleb said, "Let's go! We will conquer the giants." Choose words from the list to fill the blanks in the rest of the story.

die	conquer	giants	forty
divided	refused	desert	property

The Jews _____ to go into their new land. God made them stay in the _____ for _____ years, until all those adults were dead. Joshua and Caleb did not _____. Joshua led the Jews to _____ their enemies in Canaan. Then they divided the land so that each person had _____. Caleb fought alongside Joshua. When the land was _____, he said the words above. _____ lived on his land. "I will drive them out," he said. How old was he then?

Solve the math problem to find out his age.
When he spied the land, he was (4x10) ____ years old.
He stayed in the desert for ____ years.
He fought enemies in Canaan for (12−9+2) ____ years.
How old was he? ____ years old. (add together)

Answers: refused, desert, forty, die, conquer, divided, property, giants
40, 5, 40, 85

My Name:

Caleb's Obstacles

Caleb had to tackle all sorts of obstacles before he could live on his own land in peace. He knew he was doing what God wanted, so he kept on going. In the maze on these two pages, take Caleb through each of his obstacles and on to the next one. Pick up letters as you go and write them in the blanks below.

Caleb came through every obstacle and finally got his own land, because he believed in the Lord

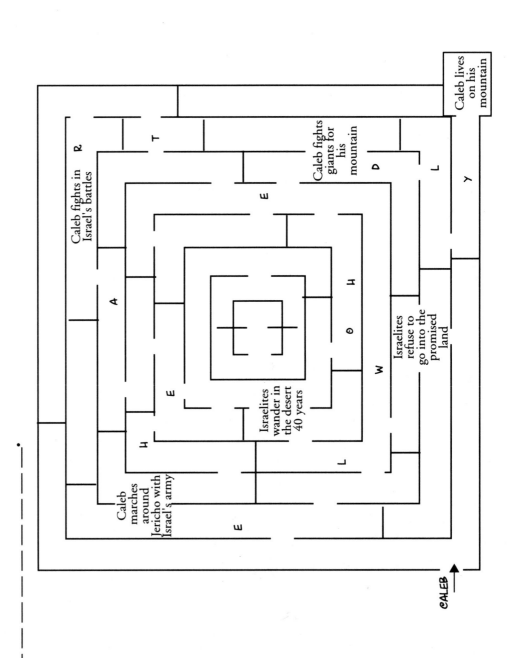

You Can Have Victory

Endure hardship with us like a good soldier of Christ Jesus.
2 Timothy 2:3

Fill in the blanks by using the code.

1	2	3	4	5	6	7	8	9	10	11	12	13	14	15
E	I	G	J	U	C	R	H	D	V	L	O	S	T	Y

If you are a Christian, you are a soldier in the army of

___ ___ ___ ___ ___ Jesus. Your worst enemy is the
6 8 7 2 13 14

___ ___ ___ ___ ___. Against him, you are like Gideon's
9 1 10 2 11

little army against the host of Midianites. Who gave

Gideon's army the victory? ___ ___ ___. When the devil
3 12 9

throws his flaming arrows (temptations) at you, hold

up the ___ ___ ___ ___ ___ ___ of faith by trusting
13 8 2 1 11 9

___ ___ ___ to help you say, "No." He will give you
4 1 13 5 13

___ ___ ___ ___ ___ ___ over the ___ ___ ___ ___ ___.
10 2 6 14 12 7 15   9 1 10 2 11

Answers: Christ, devil, faith,
shield, Jesus, victory, God,
devil

•••••••••••••••••••••••••••••••••••••

My Worship Bulletin AGES 7-11

A Mighty Warrior

Memory Verse:
Judges 6:4 *They camped on the land and ruined the crops…and did not spare a living thing for Israel, neither sheep nor cattle nor donkeys.*

Using the code, fill in the blanks in the sentences.
(Example: 1,4 = D) Answer is on next page.

	1	2	3	4
1	D	L	I	T	G
2	M	N	S	A	R
3	E	O	C	U	Y

The enemies that invaded Israel's land were the

___ ___ ___ ___ ___ ___ ___ ___. They
2,4 1,6 1,4 1,6 2,7 2,5 1,6 1,7 3,4 2,6

covered Israel's land with their tents and their livestock like

swarms of ___ ___ ___ ___ ___ ___ ___ ___.
1,5 3,5 3,6 3,7 2,6 1,7 2,6

God allowed these enemies to come because most of the Jews

were worshipping ___ ___ ___ ___ ___ ___. One man
1,6 1,4 3,5 1,5 2,6

loved God and worshipped him. God called him a "mighty

warrior." His name was G___ ___ ___ ___ ___ ___ ___. The Son
1,6 1,4 3,4 3,5 2,5

of God came to this man in the form of an

___ ___ ___ ___ ___ ___.
2,7 2,5 1,8 3,4 1,5

My Name: ___

89

Whose Army Won the Victory?

This can be nothing other than the sword of Gideon son of Joash, the Israelite. God has given the Midianites and the whole camp into his hands.
Judges 7:14

Fill in the blanks by choosing words from the list. You will use some words more than once.

signal	camp	ran	trumpets	Gideon	army
torches	Lord	jars	surrounded	victory	God

At night, G_____ and his _____ sneaked up on the _____ of their enemies and _____ it. They carried empty _____ with _____ inside in one hand and _____ in the other hand. At Gideon's _____, they smashed their _____, and their _____ shone brightly. They blew their _____ and shouted, "A _____ for the _____ and for G_____!" Their enemies woke up and _____, crying out as they fled. _____ gave G_____ and his _____ a great _____.

How Many Soldiers?

The Lord said to Gideon, "You have too many men for me to deliver Midian into their hands. In order that Israel may not boast against me that her own strength has saved her.
Judges 7:2

Solve the math problems to find out how many men fought against the enemy with Gideon.

At first, (20,000 + 10,000 + 2,000) _____ men came to fight. God said that all who were afraid must leave. (10,000 – 5,000 + 12,000 + 5,000) _____ men went home. Now there were _____ men left. God said that was still too many men. He told Gideon to take the men to the water and have them drink. Those who got down on their knees to drink had to leave. Those who did this were (10,000 – 1,000 + 700) _____ men. God chose the men who lapped water like a dog. They went to fight the enemy. There were (500 – 400 + 200) _____ soldiers who fought under Gideon's leadership.

John the Baptist's Clothes and Food

In the puzzle, start at the arrow. Print the letter "C" in the first blank. After that, count every fifth letter clockwise around the square and print the letters in the blanks.

1. From what material were John the Baptist's clothes made?

— — — — — — — — — — —

2. What was his belt made of? — — — — — — —

3. What did he eat? — — — — — — and

— — — — — .

C	H	D	I	S	A	E	H	R	T	M	R
U											O
A											L
T											S
Y	C	H	I	A	E	O	L	W	E	N	L

When Jesus began His ministry, John the Baptist said, "He must become greater; I must become less." Are you willing to put Jesus first in your life, so He is greater than you are?

Answers: locusts, wild honey, camel hair, leather

My Worship Bulletin AGES 7-11
. . . .

A Birth Announcement

Memory Verse:
Luke 1:13 *The angel said to him: "Do not be afraid, Zechariah; your prayer has been heard. Your wife Elizabeth will bear you a son."*

. . . .

In this story, underline the correct words of the choices given.
Fit those words into the puzzle.

Zechariah was a priest in the (garage, temple) of the Lord. Zechariah and Elizabeth had loved God for many years and (obeyed, disobeyed) God's commandments. They were (old, young) and had no (pigs, children). One day Zechariah saw an (uncle, angel) standing in the temple, who (sang, said), "Zechariah, you will have a (son, kitten). He will be a (trouble, joy) to you. He will bring many (people, elephants) to the Lord. To prove this is true, you will not be able to (cough, speak) until the (birth, death) of your son."

↓

— O — ↓

— — D — — Y — —

C — — — — — — G — —

— N P — — — — — L —

— — — — K

— — — H

Reading down from the arrows, what did people call this son of Zechariah? — — — — the — — — — —

My Name: —————

91

The Message of John the Baptist

He came as a witness to testify concerning that light, so that through him all men might believe
John 1:7

John the Baptist was talking about Jesus in the last sentence on the opposite page. What else did he say about Him?

Fill in the blanks with the numbered letters from the previous puzzle.

"___ ___ k, ___ ___ ___ ___ m ___ ___ G___ ___,
10 8 8   6 7 3   10 2   1   8 12   8 9

___ ___ ___ k ___ ___ ___ ___ y ___ ___ ___
11 7 8   6 2   313   2 112   6 7 3

___ ___ ___ ___ ___ ___ ___ ___ ___ ___!"
13 14 4   8 12   6 7 3   11 8 5 10 9

The Work of John the Baptist

There came a man who was sent from God; his name was John.
John 1:6

John the Baptist prepared the way for Jesus' coming. To complete this story, first fill in the missing letter from each word in the word list. Then use each word in the story below.

Word List

_re_are   S_irit   Ba_tist   _ro_het   _eo_le
_reached   re_ent   _owerful   ba_tized   _aths

John the ___ ___ ___ ___ ___ ___ ___, at the Jordan River,
     1   13

"___ ___ ___ ___ ___ ___ ___ ___ of sin.
 2   3   4

___ ___ ___ ___ ___ ___ the way for the Lord. Make
       5

straight ___ ___ ___ ___ ___ for him." Isaiah, a
        6 7

___ ___ ___ ___ ___ ___ ___, wrote that John the Baptist
  8

would come.   John ___ ___ ___ ___ ___ ___ ___ ___
                   9

many ___ ___ ___ ___ ___ in the Jordan River. "One more
      10

___ ___ ___ ___ ___ ___ ___ than I will come," he said.
 11   12

"He will baptize you with the Holy ___ ___ ___ ___ ___ ___."
                         14

92

Are You Growing?

Jesus, as a child, is an example to you of how you should grow. Do you try to grow as Jesus did? Name some ways in which you are growing. (Don't forget to ask Jesus to help you grow!)

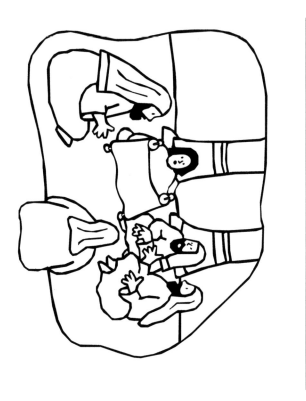

My Worship Bulletin AGES 7-11

Jesus' Boyhood

Memory Verse:
Luke 2:51 *He...was obedient to them.*

Jesus' behavior when He was young is a good example of how children should behave. The verse above says He was obedient to "them," meaning His parents. What else did Jesus do when He was a boy growing up? Find the word that does not belong on each growth chart and write it in the verse below on the numbered blank where it belongs.

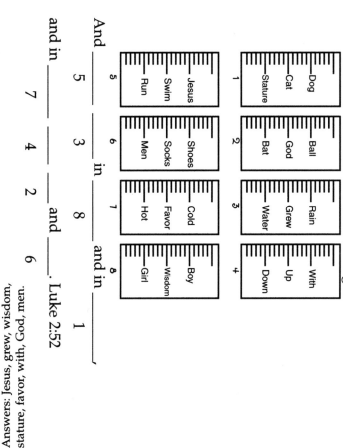

And _____ _____ in _____ _____ and in _____ ,
    5   6   7   8   1

and in _____ _____ _____ and _____ . Luke 2:52
       7   4   2   6

My Name: _____

Answers: Jesus; stature, wisdom, favor, grew, with, God, man.

In the Temple

To discover what Jesus was doing in the temple, fill the blanks with words from the word bank. Some words do not belong in the story.

Word Bank

questions	jokes	courts	heard
teachers	monkeys	sitting	listening
amazed	tomorrow	rain	understanding

Jesus was _____ in the _____ among the _____, _____ to them and asking them _____. Everyone who _____ Him was _____ at His _____ and His answers.

Jesus' Trip to Jerusalem

Every year his parents went to Jerusalem for the Feast of the Passover.
Luke 2:41

The following story tells what happened one year when Jesus and His parents went to Jerusalem for the feast. Fit the words in all capital letters into the crossword puzzle below.

When JESUS was TWELVE years OLD, He TOOK a TRIP with Mary and Joseph. They WENT to JERUSALEM to a FEAST. After traveling one day toward home, Mary and Joseph could not FIND Jesus. They looked for HIM in Jerusalem for THREE days. Then they found Him IN the TEMPLE with the teachers. He was LISTENING to them and asking QUESTIONS.

94

After Jesus' Baptism

In the Scripture below, some words are in all capital letters. Find and circle them in the word search puzzle. You may go down, across and diagonally. Some words share letters. (Circle the two "I's" last.)

As soon as Jesus was BAPTIZED, HE went up out of the WATER. At that MOMENT HEAVEN was OPENED, and HE SAW the SPIRIT of GOD DESCENDING like a DOVE and LIGHTING on Him. And a VOICE from heaven said, "This IS MY SON, WHOM I LOVE; WITH HIM I AM WELL PLEASED." — Matthew 3:16-17

```
D E S C E N D I N G W
H W L M O M E N T L I
E E V O I C E H E I T
S L I H V I I S O G H
P L E A S E D N P H W
I S H I M G O D E T H
R O A H E A V E N I O
I N I W A T E R E N M
T B A P T I Z E D G Y
```

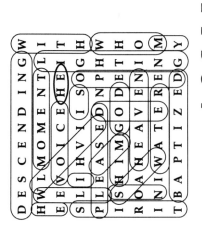

My Worship Bulletin AGES 7-11
: ....

John Announces the Promised One

Memory Verse:
Matthew 3:1 *John the Baptist came, preaching in the Desert of Judea.*

....

People came from miles around to hear John preach. He baptized those who repented of their sins. "Are you the one God promised to send?" some people asked. To read John's answer, cross out all the K's and V's. Then write the remaining letters on the blanks below and separate them into words.

"KKIVVBKAPTVIKZVVEKYVOKKUVWIKTVKHVVWAKK-
TVEKRKFOVVRKKKKREVPENTVWANKKCEVBUKT-
VAVFVTKERKKMVEKWIKKLLVCVOVMVEKONEVK-
WHKOVIKSMVORKEKVPOKWERVVFULKTHKANVKIK-
WHVOSESAKNVDALSKIKAMVVNOKTKFIVTV-
TOKCKARKRYVHEKKWVILVLKBVAPKTIKZVEKVKKKYK-
OUVWIKKTHVKTHKEVVVHOKLLYVSPKKIRVITK."

My Name: _____

_____

_____

Answer: I baptize you with water for repentance. But after me will come one who is more powerful than I, whose sandals I am not fit to carry. He will baptize you with the Holy Spirit.

95

Jesus' Reply to Temptations

Shade in all of the even-numbered shapes to find the word to fill the blank.

What did Jesus say to each temptation of the devil? _____ .

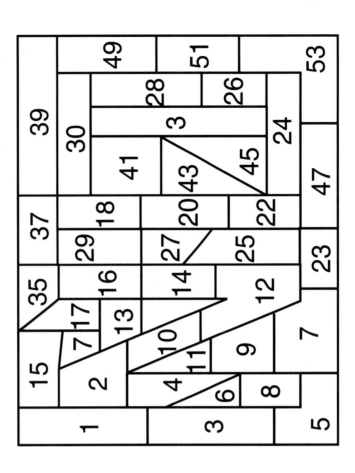

98

Jesus' Temptation

He was in the desert forty days, being tempted by Satan. He was with the wild animals, and angels attended him.

Mark 1:13

Following these days, the devil tempted Jesus three more times. After each temptation, Jesus quoted a _____ from the

_____ .
second word   first word

To find the words to fill the two blanks, print the missing letter on each line in the two sets below.

First set:

T U W X Y Z: ____

A B C D F G: ____

Q S T U V W: ____

O P Q R T U: ____

D F G H I J: ____

Second set:

A C D E F G: ____

G H J K L M: ____

Y Z A C D E: ____

I J K M N O: ____

C D F G H I: ____

Come, Follow Me

Whoever serves me must follow me; and where I am, my servant also will be. My Father will honor the one who serves me.
John 12:26

Jesus says to each person, "Come, follow Me." He wants sinners to believe in Him as Savior. He wants Christians to follow Him and do what He would do in every action. Are you following Him?

Write what you can do to follow Jesus:

____

____

____

Write what you might do that would not be following Jesus:

____

____

____

My Worship Bulletin AGES 7-11

Jesus Chooses 12 Disciples

Memory Verse:

Matthew 4:19 *I will make you fishers of men.*

Jesus chose 12 men to be His special disciples. They traveled with Him and helped Him in His work. Four were fishermen when Jesus called them. From then on, He said they would fish for men, not fish. He meant that they would lead people to Jesus. What two words did Jesus say when He called the men to be his disciples? Find the letters on the fish and put them in correct order on the blanks.

"_ _ _ _ _ _   _ _."

Answer: Follow Me.

My Name: ______________________________

The Disciples Follow Jesus

"Come, follow Me," Jesus said. In the puzzle, take the disciples to Jesus. First, mark an "X" on the names of the Bible characters who were not one of the 12 disciples. Begin at the arrow and move either right, left, up, or down (not diagonally) until you have all the disciples coming to Jesus.

Begin →

JOHN	JAMES 1	NOAH	ADAM	MOSES	AARON
JOSHUA	JUDAS	PETER	PHILIP	DANIEL	DAVID
MARK	PAUL	ABEL	MATTHEW	THOMAS	JOSEPH
ENOCH	JONAH	JOB	CAIN	SIMON	SHEM
HAM	JAPHETH	SOLOMON	THADDAEUS	JAMES 2	SAUL
ISAIAH	JEREMIAH	LUKE	ANDREW	BARTHOLOMEW	JESUS

→ **End**

The Names of Jesus' Disciples

He called his disciples to him and chose twelve of them, whom he also designated apostles.
Luke 6:13

The 12 men whom Jesus named are listed below. Two had the name James. Can you fit the names into the puzzle? (Hint: Begin with the longest word first, then do the second and third longest.)

Matthew   Thomas   Andrew

Thaddaeus   Peter   James

John   Judas   James

Bartholomew   Philip   Simon

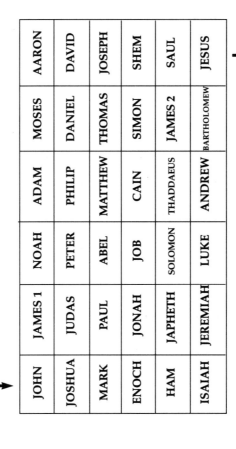

100

Giving Thanks

Supply the missing vowels in the verse below to find what God wants us to do.

__lw __ys g __ v __ng th __nks t __ G __d th __ F __th __r

f __ r __ v __ r th __ ng, __ n th __ n __ m __ __ f __ __ r

L __ rd J __ s __ s Chr __ st. Ephesians 5:20

List some things for which you thank God:

_____

_____

_____

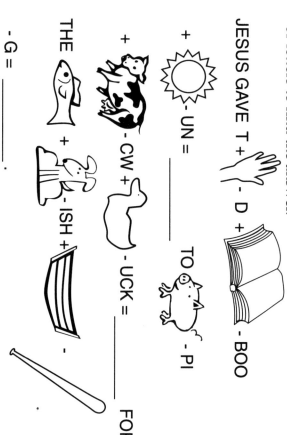

Do you thank God before eating your meals? Do you thank Him for everything?

Answer: Always giving thanks to God the Father for everything in the name of our Lord Jesus Christ.

What Jesus Did Before Eating

Memory Verse:
Matthew 14:15 *As evening approached, the disciples came to him and said, "This is a remote place, and it's already getting late. Send the crowds away, so they can go to the villages and buy themselves some food."*

The story of how Jesus fed hungry people is inside. What did Jesus do first before He fed the people? Add or subtract words or letters to find the answer.

JESUS GAVE T + 🤚 - D + 📖 - BOO

+ ☀ - UN = _____

+ 🐄 - CW + 🐰 - UCK = _____

THE + 🐟 + 🐕 - ISH + 🏏 - _____ FOR

- G = _____ .

My Name: _____

Answer: Jesus gave thanks to God for the food.

101

Jesus Calms a Storm

That day when evening came, he said to his disciples,
"Let us go over to the other side."
Mark 4:35

What happened to Jesus and the disciples on the sea that night?
In each pair of words, choose the correct word and write it on
the blanks below, beside its sentence number.

1. Jesus and His disciples were on a (boat, bike) on the (way, sea)
of Galilee. 2. A big (squall, salmon) came up. 3. Jesus was
(scared, asleep). 4. The disciples were (afraid, daring) and asked
Jesus to (push, help) them. 5. Jesus spoke to the (moon, wind)
and the (waves, fish). 6. The sea became (rough, balmy).

1. __ __ __ __ , __ __ __ .
   1 2 3 4   5 6 7

2. __ __ __ __ .
   8 9 10

3. __ __ __ .
     11

4. __ __ __ , __ __ __ __ .
          12 13 14

5. __ __ , __ __ __ __ __ .
   15   16   17

6. __ __ __ .
  18 19

Fill the blanks with the numbered letters from the opposite
page:

Jesus said to the wind and waves, " __ __ __ __ __ __ !
                                    8 9 12 6 4

__ __ __ __ __ __ !" The disciples said, " __ __ __
1 6   5 4 12 10 10   15 14 2

__ __ __ __ __ __ ? __ __ __ __
12 5   4 14 12 5   6 17 6 16 4 14 6

__ __ __ __ __ __ __ __ __ __ __
15 12 16 13   3 16 13   4 14 6   15 3 17 6 5

__ __ __ __ __ __ !"
2 1 6 19   14 12 18

Answer: "Quiet! Be
still!" "Who is this?
Even the wind and
the waves obey
Him!"

Answers:
1. boat, sea;
2. squall;
3. asleep;
4. afraid, help;
5. wind, waves;
6. balmy

Be Thankful

Write in the correct vowels in this verse about being thankful:

_nt_r h_s g_t_s w_th th_nksg_v_ng

_nd h_s c__rts w_th pr__s_; g_v_

th_nks t_ h_m _nd pr__s_ h_s

n_m_.

— Psalm 100:4

What special words of thanks do you want to tell Jesus? Write them for the lips to say.

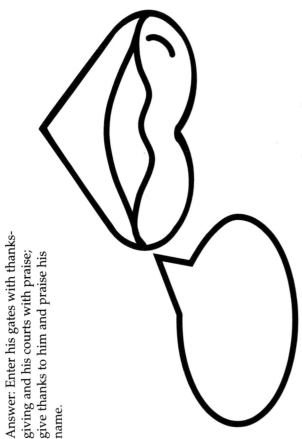

Answer: Enter his gates with thanksgiving and his courts with praise;
give thanks to him and praise his
name.

Jesus Heals Some Lepers

Memory Verse:

Luke 17:12-13 *They stood at a distance and called out in a loud voice, "Jesus, Master, have pity on us!"*

The men who called to Jesus had a dreadful disease called "leprosy." It is a contagious disease. In Bible times, anyone with leprosy could not come close to other people. They could not even live in their own houses or towns. Choose the correct numbers from below to fill in the blanks in the sentences that tell the story of the lepers.

1   9   10

1. ___ lepers lived outside a town.
2. ___ lepers could not go into town.
3. Jesus passed by. ___ lepers called, "Jesus, have pity on us!"
4. Jesus told the ___ lepers, "Go show yourselves to the priest."
5. ___ lepers started to go.
6. As they went, ___ lepers were healed.
7. ___ of the lepers came back and thanked Jesus.
8. ___ did not come back to thank Jesus.
9. Jesus asked, "Were not all ___ cleansed? Where are the other ___?"
10. Jesus was glad that ___ man thanked Him. He was sorry that ___ men did not.

Answers: 10, 10, 10, 10, 10, 10, 1, 9, 10, 1, 9.

My Name: _____

105

The Heart That Pleases Jesus

Unscramble the letters in the heart to find the word to print in the blanks.

Jesus wants us all to have _____ hearts. If

we truly do, we will have _____ lips, too.

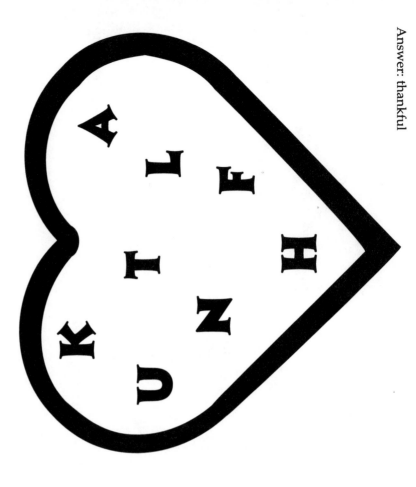

The Man Who Pleased Jesus

Choose words from the list to finish each line of this poem:

fine   then   please   men

around   disease   ground   nine

Ten lepers cried out to the Lord,

"Oh, help us, will you _____?"

For we are full of leprosy,

A terrible _____."

"Go to the temple, to the priest,"

The Master said right _____;

And as they went, they all were healed —

All ten poor leprous _____.

Nine hurried off to find their homes,

But one turned right _____;

He came to Jesus, and he kneeled

Before Him on the _____.

He cried aloud, "I thank You, Lord,

For now I am so _____."

And Jesus said, "Were not ten healed?

Where are the other _____?"

Two Houses

In the top squares, draw the two houses and foundations. Above each, write the kind of builder who would build that house. Draw storms beating on the houses. In the lower squares, draw what happened to each house.

_____ Builder   _____ Builder

Is your house built on the Rock, Christ Jesus? _____

My Name: _____

Two Houses

Memory Verse:

Matthew 7:28-29 *When Jesus had finished saying these things, the crowds were amazed at his teaching, because he taught as one who had authority, and not as their teachers of the law.*

In Jesus' parables, He told about two houses, two ways and two gates. The story about the houses is on the front and back of this bulletin. The sayings about the ways and gates are inside the bulletin. Unscramble the words to fill in the blanks in Jesus' story:

"Every one who hears these words of mine and puts them into practice is like a _____ (cork). The _____ (isew) man who built his _____ (sheou) on the _____ (anri) came down, the _____ (tramess) rose, and the _____ (diwns) blew and beat against that _____ (sheou); yet it did not fall, because it had its foundation on the _____ (cork).

"But everyone who hears these words of mine and does not put them into practice is like a _____ (shoolfi) man who built his _____ (sheou) on the _____ (nads). The _____ (anri) came down, the _____ (tramess) rose, and the _____ (diwns) blew and beat against that _____ (sheou), and it fell with a great crash."

Answers: wise, house, rock, rain, streams, winds, house, rock, foolish, house, sand, rain, streams, winds, house.

Two Gates and Two Roads

Enter through the narrow gate. For wide is the gate and broad is the road that leads to destruction, and many enter through it. But small is the gate and narrow the road that leads to life, and only a few find it.
Matthew 7:13-14

Jesus doesn't want us to go to destruction (hell), but He does want us to go to life (heaven). That's why, in the above verses, He tells us to get on the road that leads to life.

Using the code, fill in the blanks in Jesus' words below to learn how to get on the road that leads to life.

1	T	F	R	I
2	A	U	H	E
3	L	Y	W	M
	4	5	6	7

Jesus answered, "I am the ___ ___ ___ ___ and the ___ ___ ___
1,4 1,6 2,5 1,4 2,6   3,6 2,4 3,5

and the ___ ___ ___ ___. No one
       3,4 1,7 1,5 2,7

comes to the ___ ___ ___ ___ ___ ___ ___ except through
             1,5 2,4 1,4, 2,6 2,7 1,6

___ ___." John 14:6
3,7 2,7

In the Scripture at the top of the opposite page, find the words to fill in the blanks in the drawing below. Print "Jesus" on the way that leads from the bottom road to the top one. On which road are you? If you have asked Jesus to be your Savior, you are on the road that leads to life (heaven!).

HEAVEN

ROAD

N

L ___

S ___ GATE

J

B ___ WAY

D ___

W ___ GATE

A Handy Gospel

God's Word includes the Gospel. Write these words and Scripture references on the fingers of the hand. Quietly look up the verses in your Bible.

1. I have sinned. Romans 3:23
2. God loves me. John 3:16
3. Jesus died for my sins. 1 Corinthians 15:3
4. I believe in Jesus. Acts 16:31
5. I am saved. Romans 10:13

Have you heard and believed the Gospel and received Jesus as your Savior? _____

My Worship Bulletin AGES 7-11

The Farmer and the Seed

Memory Verse:
Matthew 13:3 *Then he told them many things in parables, saying, "A farmer went out to sow his seed."*

Jesus told the story of a farmer who scattered seed on his land. It fell in four kinds of places. What were they? Use the code to fill the blanks.

	1	2	3	4
A	A	C	D	E
B	G	H	I	K
C	L	N	O	P
D	R	S	T	Y

The seed fell:

1. On a __ __ __ __
   B,2 A,1 D,1 A,3

2. On __ __ __ __ __ __ __
   D,1 C,3 A,2 B,4   D,4 C,4 C,1   A,1 D,3 B,2

3. Among __ __ __ __ __ __
   D,3 B,2 C,3 D,1 C,2 D,2

4. In __ __ __ __ __ __ __.
   B,1 C,3 C,3   D,2 C,3 B,3 C,1

Answer:
1. hard path
2. rocky places
3. thorns
4. good soil

My Name: _____

109

Match each number from the sentences on the opposite page to the picture that represents its meaning.

I love
God's Word.

I believe
in Jesus.

TROUBLE!

TROUBLE!
TROUBLE!

JESUS

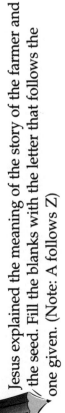

The Meaning of Jesus' Story

Jesus explained the meaning of the story of the farmer and the seed. Fill the blanks with the letter that follows the one given. (Note: A follows Z)

1. The seed is the __ __ __ __ of God (the Bible).
   V n q c

2. The soil is a person's __ __ __ __ __.
   g d z q s

3. The hard path is a person who hears the Word but does not understand and receive it. He has a hard __ __ __ __ __.
   g d z q s

4. The birds who snatch away the seed stand for the
   __ __ __ __ __.
   c d u h k

5. The person whose seed falls on rocky places says he believes the Word, but he really doesn't. He falls away because he has many __ __ __ __ __ __ __ __ __.
   s q n t a k d r

6. The one whose seed fell among thorns lets the seed get choked by too little or too much __ __ __ __ __.
   l n m d x

7. The person who received the seed on good ground receives the __ __ __ __ and believes in __ __ __ __ __.
   v n q c   I d r t r

How to Put Treasures in Heaven

Can you fill in the blanks in the sentences about storing up treasures in heaven? These are some of the ways you can store them up. Maybe you will think of more.

1. Read the _____ every day and do what it says.
2. Win _____ to Jesus.
3. _____ money to the Lord's work.
4. Bow your head and _____ to Jesus every day.
5. Confess any _____ to Jesus that you know you have committed.
6. Go to _____ and learn more about Jesus.
7. Be _____, even to those who treat you badly.

Doing these things will store up treasures in heaven for you. When you get there, Jesus will reward you for all you have done to please Him.

Answers: Bible, souls, give, pray, sins, church, kind

The Root of All Evil

Memory Verse:
1 Timothy 6:6 *Godliness with contentment is great gain.*

Have you ever heard the statement, "Money is the root of all evil"? The Bible does not say that. Go through the maze, following the letters, THE ROOT OF ALL EVIL IS until you reach the correct answer.

The root of all evil is _____ _____ _____.

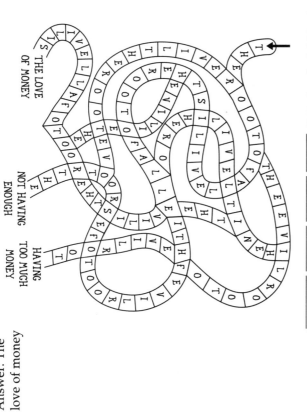

THE LOVE OF MONEY

NOT HAVING ENOUGH MONEY

HAVING TOO MUCH MONEY

Answer: The love of money

My Name: _____

111

Where to Store Your Treasures

Where is the safest place to store your treasures? Unscramble the letters in the words following the blanks to find out.

Jesus said, "Do not store up for yourselves _____

(astrurees) on _____ (heart), where _____

(thom) and _____ (stur) destroy, and where

_____ (viethes) break in and _____ (least). But

store up for yourselves _____ (asturees) in

_____ (haveen), where _____ (thom) and

(stur) do not destroy, and where _____ (viethes)

do not break in and _____ (least). For where your

_____ (asturee) is, there your _____ (thare) will

be also." Matthew 6:19-21

A Question Jesus Asked

Loving money can cause a person to do anything to get it. He may steal, cheat, lie or kill. He may never trust Jesus as his Savior. Write the question that Jesus asked about money on the blanks below. Find the correct words on the numbered coins.

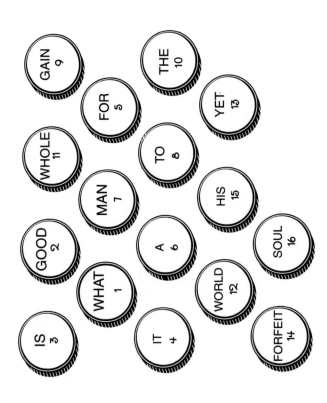

GAIN 9 · THE 10 · FOR 5 · YET 13 · WHOLE 11 · TO 8 · MAN 7 · HIS 15 · GOOD 2 · A 6 · SOUL 16 · WHAT 1 · IS 3 · WORLD 12 · IT 4 · FORFEIT 14

___ ___ ___ ___ ___ ___ ___ ___
1   2   3   4   5   6   7   8

___ ___ ___ ___ ___ ___
9   10 11 12 13 14

___ ___ ? Mark 8:36
15 16

112

My Promise to God

Will you promise God to do your best to be in Sunday school each Sunday? If so, sign your name here:

_____

Name some activities that you do in your Sunday school:

1. _____

2. _____

3. _____

4. _____

5. _____

Circle the one you like to do best.

Do you thank God for your Sunday school teacher and other workers?

Will you thank them for taking the time to study the Bible and teach it to you?

My Worship Bulletin AGES 7-11

Sunday School Kickoff

Memory Verse:

Psalm 122:1 *I rejoiced with those who said to me, "Let us go to the house of the Lord."*

You might want to go to church, but many things and people can tempt you to stay away. Find a way to get to church, avoiding all the temptations. Start at the arrow.

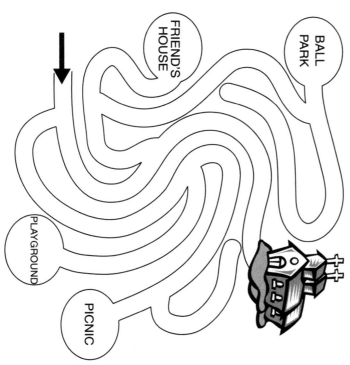

My Name: _____

What Is a Name for the Bible?

From the first puzzle on the opposite page, print each circled letter in the blank that has its number in the second puzzle.

$\overline{1}$ $\overline{2}$ $\overline{3}$

$\overline{3}$ $\overline{4}$ $\overline{3}$ $\overline{5}$ $\overline{6}$ $\overline{7}$ $\overline{8}$ $\overline{1}$ $\overline{9}$ $\overline{10}$ $\overline{11}$

$\overline{12}$ $\overline{13}$ $\overline{13}$ $\overline{14}$.

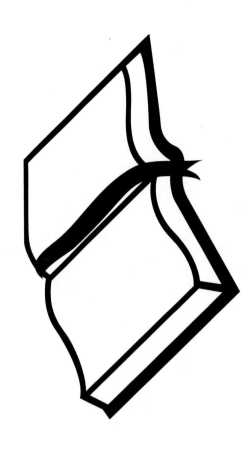

What to Do With a Bible

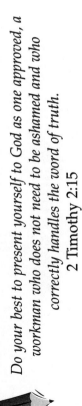

Do your best to present yourself to God as one approved, a workman who does not need to be ashamed and who correctly handles the word of truth.
2 Timothy 2:15

What book do we study when we go to Sunday school?

The _____.

Print in the blanks the letters that follow the letters given. (A follows Z.)

What does God want you to do with the Bible?

$\underset{Q\ d\ z\ c}{\overset{3\ 7}{\bigcirc\bigcirc}}$ it every day. $\underset{R\ s\ t\ c\ x}{\overset{8\ 1}{\bigcirc\bigcirc}}$ it often.

$\underset{L\ d\ l\ n\ q\ h\ y\ d}{\overset{5\ 9}{\bigcirc\bigcirc}}$ many verses.

$\underset{A\ d\ k\ h\ d\ u\ d}{\overset{12\ 6\ 4}{\bigcirc\bigcirc\bigcirc}}$ every word. $\underset{N\ a\ d\ x}{\overset{13}{\bigcirc}}$ it.

$\underset{K\ n\ u\ d}{\bigcirc}$ it more than gold or silver.

$\underset{S\ g\ z\ m\ j}{\overset{2\ 10\ 14}{\bigcirc\bigcirc}}\ \underset{F\ n\ c}{\overset{11}{\bigcirc}}$ for it.

114

My Worship Bulletin AGES 7-11

Happy Thanksgiving

Memory Verse:
Psalm 45:2 *Let us come before him with thanksgiving and extol him with music and song.*

....

If God asked you to give Him a gift, would you give it? How often? Use the code to find one special gift God wants from His children. Example: 11 = S. The answers are on the next page.

A	C	E	F	I	L	N	O	P	R	S	T	U	Y
1	2	3	4	5	6	7	8	9	10	11	12	13	14

1. The Israelites gave God the first sheaves of wheat from their harvest, called the

— — — — — — —
4　5　10　11　12　4　10

2. Our special gift to God is found in Hebrews 13:15: "Let us

offer to God a — — — — — — —
2　8　7　12　5　7　13

— — — — — — — — the fruit of
1　2　10　5　4　6　6　14

— — — — — — — — — of
9　10　1　5　11　3

— — — — — — — — that
10　1　5　11　3

confess his name."

My Name: _____

My Thanksgiving to God

....

Always giving thanks to God the Father for everything, in the name of our Lord Jesus Christ.
Ephesians 5:20

Below is a list of a few things for which to thank God. Fit them into the puzzle.

Jesus	friends	sunshine	parents
prayer	kinfolk	church	rain
God	love	good	Bible

— — — — — T — —

— — — H — —

— — — A — —

— — N — —

— K — — — —

— S — — — —

G — — the FATHER

— I — —

— V — —

— I — —

— N — —

— G — —

— — FOOD

Don't forget to thank God for His gifts to you!

Answer: PARENTS, CHURCH, PRAYER, RAIN, KINFOLK, JESUS, GOD THE FATHER, FRIENDS, LOVE, BIBLE, SUNSHINE, GOOD FOOD

Thank God for His Special Gift

Thanks be to God for his indescribable gift!
2 Corinthians 9:15

Write in the add-a-letter pyramid the words you wrote in the puzzle on the opposite page.

Have you received Jesus as your Savior? Do you thank God for His gift of eternal life? Each sentence below tells something about this gift. Unscramble the missing words and write them in the blanks. The first one is just one letter.

1. Jesus said, " _____ _____ am the way and the truth and the life."

2. Believe _____ (ni) the Lord Jesus, and you will be saved.

3. The wages of _____ (ins) is death, but the gift of God is eternal life.

4. _____ (gnis) to the Lord and praise His name.

5. When we have the gift of eternal life, we can say, "Where, O death, is your _____ (ginst)?"

6. If we do not thank God for this gift, we are _____ (tigyns).

Immanuel

From the list, choose words to fill in the blanks in the poem.
("Immanuel" means "God with us.")

| man | dwell | divine | earth |
| birth | plan | Immanuel | mine |

It was God who came to _____

By the way of virgin _____ ;

God, the Son, became a _____

And fulfilled the Father's _____ .

Some doubt He was _____ ;

But they can't shake this faith of _____ .

God, the Son, came to _____

"God with us": _____ .

Answers: earth, birth, man, plan
divine, mine, dwell, Immanuel

Advent

Memory Verse:

Luke 2:10 *The angel answered,... "The holy one to be born will be called the Son of God."*

In the puzzle below, write the letter that is missing from the second word in each pair. Place the letters in order to fill the blanks and finish the sentences. Answers are on the next page.

When the angel told Mary she was to be the mother of God's son, she said, "I am the Lord's

_____ _____ _____ _____ ."

In BASTE but not in BEAT: __
In TEAM but not in MAT: __
In PART but not in TAP: __
In AVERT but not in RATE: __
In CHAIN but not in CHIN: __
In PRINCE but not in PRICE: __
In BITTER but not in TRIBE: __

When the angel told Joseph that God wanted him to marry Mary, Joseph _____ _____ _____ _____ _____

In BOAT but not in TAB: __
In TABLE but not in LATE: __
In ENTER but not in RENT: __
In NAVY but not in VAN: __
In DOPE but not in POD: __
In DEPOT but not in POET: __

My Name: _____

A Special Visitor

To fill in the blanks on this page and the opposite page, find the letter in the circle or circles with the same number that is under the blank. Example: 3,4 = J.

Circles: N L A J O R E B S W Y F I M H G P U
1 2 3 4 5 6 7 8 9 10

One day ___ ___ ___ sent the ___ ___ ___ ___ ___
9 4,5 2   2,3 1 9 5 1,2

to ___ ___ ___ ___ ___ ___ ." "Do
9 2,3 3 4 6 5 1,2   8 2,3 4 7

not be ___ ___ ___ ___ ___ ___ ," he said. "God will
2,3 7,8 4 2,3 6 2

give you a ___ ___ ___ . He will be ___ ___ ___ ___
3 2,3 3   7 4,5 3 7

the ___ ___ ___ of the Most ___ ___ ___ ." Mary ___ ___ ___
5,6 4,5 1   8,9 6 9 8,9

said, ___ ___ ___ it be as you have ___ ___ ___ ___ ."
8 2,3 7   5,6 2,3 6 2

Answers to front: servant, obeyed

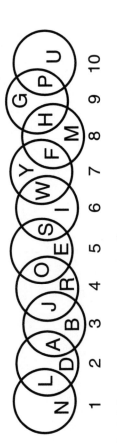

Mary was pledged to marry to ___ ___ ___ ___ ___ ___ .
3,4 4,5 5,6 5 9,10 8,9

An angel came to him in a ___ ___ ___ ___ ___ saying,
2 4 5 2,3 8

"Do not be afraid to take Mary as your ___ ___ ___ ___ .
6,7 6 7,8 5

God gave her the ___ ___ ___ ___ . Call His name
3 2,3 3 7

___ ___ ___ ___ . He will save people from their
3,4 5 5,6 10 5,6

___ ___ ___ ___ ."
5,6 6 1 5,6

Answers: God, angel, Gabriel, Mary, afraid, baby boy, Son, High, may, said, Joseph, dream, wife, baby, Jesus, sins

Dear God

Write a thank-You note to God for sending baby Jesus:

_____

_____

_____

_____

_____

_____

_____

_____

My Worship Bulletin AGES 7-11

Christmas: The Birth of Jesus

Memory Verse:

Luke 2:11 *Today in the town of David a Savior has been born to you; he is Christ the Lord.*

Choose words from the list to supply the missing words in this rhyme about Jesus' birth. The answers are on the next page.

Boy	Child	too	found	mother	head	rejoicing
bed	birth	hay	earth	say	angel	tidings
lay	'round	joy	inn	do	star	swaddling

Christmas, Christmas, Christmas! Here's what the letters ____:

C is for the Christ ____ who is in the manger ____.

H is for the cattle's ____ that pillowed Jesus' ____.

R is for ____ by those around His ____.

I is for a busy ____, where room could not be ____.

S is for the ____ cloths that wrapped the baby ____.

T is for good ____ that brought such wondrous ____.

M is for the ____ dear who watched her baby ____.

A is for the ____ host who told of peace on ____.

S is for the ____ so bright that shone at Jesus' ____.

You're wished a Merry Christmas and Happy New Year, ____.

And may you honor Jesus in everything you ____.

My Name: _____

J _____

M _____

J _____

G _____

A _____

S _____

K _____ HEROD

I _____

M _____ M _____

Who Are You?

Draw a line from the question to the picture it matches
on the opposite page. On the line beneath the picture,
write the name of the person or persons. The first letter of
each name is supplied.

1. Who was Jesus' mother?

2. Who was Jesus' true father?

3. Who married Mary?

4. Who had no room in the inn?

5. Who lay in a manger?

6. Who came to earth to tell about Jesus' birth?

7. Who heard the angel's message?

8. Who were led by a star to Jesus?

9. Who wanted to kill baby Jesus?

120

A Shiny Sign

Draw a picture of the star that shone over Bethlehem. On each point, write one of these words:

BABY JESUS HAS BEEN BORN

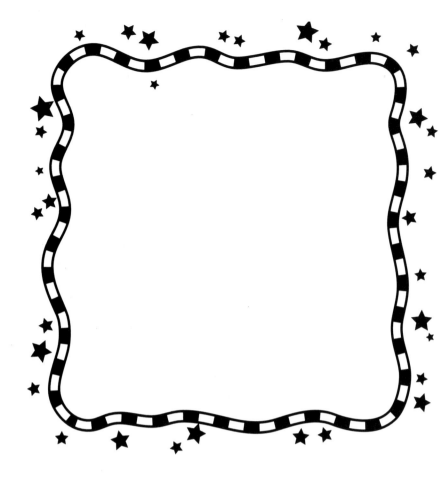

Tell this Good News to someone who may not know why you celebrate Christmas!

My Worship Bulletin AGES 7-11

Christmas: The Wise Men Visit Jesus

Memory Verse:
Matthew 2:11 *They saw the child with his mother Mary, and they bowed down and worshipped him.*

Make a path through the maze for the wise men to visit the king in Jerusalem and continue on to see Jesus. Find another way for them to go home, because an angel warned them in a dream not to go back to the king.

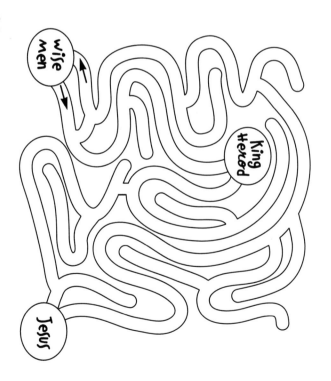

My Name: _____

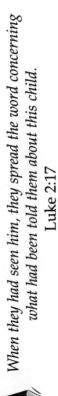

The Shepherds See Jesus

When they had seen him, they spread the word concerning what had been told them about this child.

Luke 2:17

Find all of the words in capital letters in the word search puzzle on the opposite page, going down, across or diagonally.

One NIGHT there were SHEPHERDS in the FIELDS, keeping WATCH over their FLOCKS. An ANGEL of the LORD appeared to them, and the GLORY of the Lord shone around them. They were terrified. But the angel said, "Don't be AFRAID. I bring you GOOD NEWS of great JOY that will be for all PEOPLE. Today in the TOWN of BETHLEHEM a SAVIOR has been BORN; He IS CHRIST the Lord. You will FIND a baby wrapped in swaddling clothes lying in a MANGER." Suddenly a great HEAVENLY HOST appeared with the angel, praising God and saying, "Glory to God in the highest."

When the angels left, the shepherds said, "Let's GO and SEE this thing that has happened. So they hurried off and found MARY and JOSEPH. The BABY was lying in the manger.

Write the remaining letters here: _____

Unscramble them to write some more words the angels said:
_____ on _____ .

Answer: Peace on earth.

Key to puzzle on front:

H	A	B	A	B	Y	L	O	R	D	J
E	H	E	F	L	O	C	K	S	G	O
A	O	T	I	T	O	W	N	N	A	S
V	S	H	E	P	H	E	R	D	S	E
E	T	L	L	G	L	O	R	Y	A	P
N	J	E	D	E	B	T	L	R	V	H
L	O	H	S	E	Y	E	C	G	I	P
Y	Y	E	P	R	G	H	H	O	O	E
F	N	M	A	N	G	E	R	O	R	O
I	E	M	A	F	R	A	I	D	C	P
N	W	W	A	T	C	H	S	I	E	L
D	S	T	N	I	G	H	T	S	E	E

My Gifts to Jesus

Have you given the two gifts to Jesus that are listed on the center pages? If not, will you give Him these gifts now? If you have already given Jesus these gifts, what special thing will you try to do as a gift to Him this Christmas season?

_____

_____

_____

_____

_____

_____

Christmas: Why Jesus Came

Memory Verse:

1 John 4:9 *This is how God showed his love among us: He sent his one and only Son into the world.*

. . . .

Find a path through the maze from heaven to earth and write the letters in the blanks. "The Father has sent his Son __

__ __ __ __ __ __ __ __ ." 1 John 4:14

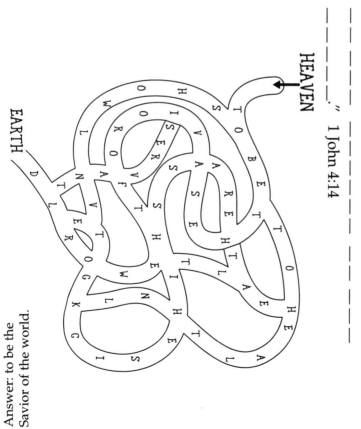

HEAVEN

EARTH

Answer: to be the
Savior of the world.

My Name: _____

Two Gifts to Jesus

At this time of year, we think of God's wonderful gift to us. He gave His Son to come into the world and be born in a human body. Jesus came to die for our sins. God will give us the gift of eternal life if we will receive Jesus as Savior. What are the two best gifts you can give to Jesus? To find the answer, use the clues to fill in the puzzles on the opposite page.

Puzzle 1

1. They kept sheep near Bethlehem.

2. He married Jesus' mother.

3. She was the mother of Jesus.

4. This led the wise men to Jesus.

5. The town where Jesus was born.

Puzzle 2

6. He told the shepherds about Jesus' birth.

7. The wise men went to _____ Herod.

8. The wise men brought these to Jesus.

9. The baby who lay in a manger.

Reading down from the arrows, fill in the blanks:

The two best gifts I can give Jesus are:

My _____ to be saved.

My _____ to serve him every day.

Puzzle One: →

1. ___ ___ ___ ___

2. ___ ___ ___

3. ___ ___ ___

4. ___ ___ ___

5. ___ ___ ___ ___

Puzzle Two: →

6. ___ ___ ___

7. ___ ___ ___

8. ___ ___ ___

9. ___ ___ ___

Answers: 1. shepherds, 2. Joseph, 3. Mary, 4. star, 5. Bethlehem, 6. angel, 7. find, 8. gifts, 9. Jesus. heart, life

My new Year's Promise

We will do everything the Lord has said.
Exodus 19:8

Make a list of some things you know God would want you to do this year.

_____

_____

_____

_____

_____

If you promise God you will do your best to do these things with His help, sign your name:

My Worship Bulletin AGES 7-11

A new Year!

Memory Verse:
Romans 12:1 *Offer your bodies as living sacrifices, holy and pleasing to God — this is your spiritual act of worship.*

Will you let God shape and mold your life this year, as a potter molds a clay pot? He will make something beautiful out of you. Write a Scripture on the pot by matching the shapes.

My Name: _____

Answer: O Lord...we are the clay, you are the potter; we are all the work of your hand. (Isaiah 64:8)

A Race for Life

Do you not know that in a race all the runners run, but only one gets the prize? Run in such a way as to get the prize.
1 Corinthians 9:24

Living our lives is like running a race. The race begins at birth and ends when life is over. Sometimes there are crooks and turns in our path, or we have uphill climbs. Other times the way is easy and downhill.

God has a prize for all of His children at the end of the race. We will receive rewards for serving Jesus and living to please Him. It's up to us to earn many rewards. If we keep our eyes on Jesus, He will guide us all the way. Will you let Him guide you this year?

On the opposite page, take the runner down the path by filling in the vowels in Hebrews 12:1-2.

126

Show Your Love

Let us not love with words or tongue but with actions and in truth.

1 John 3:18

This verse is not saying it is wrong to say, "I love you." But it is telling us to show our love by our actions. On the lines below, write the names of three persons to whom you will show your love in a special way this week.

_____

_____

_____

Valentine's Day

Memory Verse:

1 John 4:14 *We love because he first loved us.*

On Valentine's Day, we think of love. Whom should we love most of all? _____. How much should we love Him? _____

Write the correct words in the puzzle by finding the matching shapes.

YOUR SOUL YOUR

ALL STRENGTH

ALL YOUR HEART LORD YOUR

AND WITH YOUR MIND.

Luke 10:27

AND WITH ALL AND WITH ALL

LOVE THE GOD WITH

My Name: _____

Answers: Jesus;
Love the Lord your God with all your heart and with all your soul and with all your strength and with all your mind.
Luke 10:27

Love Your Neighbor

Your neighbor can be anyone — family, friends, schoolmates, people who live near you or strangers. If we truly love God, we will love other people as much as we love ourselves. Decorate all of the valentines on this page that name actions which show love for others. Cross out those that do not.

Be selfish and greedy

Help someone in need

Gladly do your chores

Be polite and courteous

Be a friend to a lonely person

Forgive those who wrong you

Say unkind words

Share your treats and toys

Argue and fight

Make fun of someone